Skiing *on a* Budget

Moneywise tips and deals on lift tickets, lodging, equipment and more.

CLAIRE WALTER

D1065772

BETTERWAY BOOKS
CINCINNATI. OHIO

DEDICATION

To Lee Carlson, *Skiing* magazine's senior travel editor, whose assignments to me were the inspiration for this book.

ABOUT THE AUTHOR

Claire Walter has been budget skiing as long as she has been skiing. She is western editor for *Skiing* magazine, writes a travel column for *Cross Country Skier* and has contributed to such other magazines as *Hemispheres, Shape* and *Travel & Leisure.* Her *Best Resorts in America* won a Lowell Thomas Award. She is the author of *The Berlitz Handbook to Skiing the Alps, The Colorado Outdoor Activity Guide* and *Rocky Mountain Skiing,* which was honored with the 1994 Harold Hirsch Award for excellence in ski books. She lives in Boulder, Colorado, with her husband, Ral Sandberg, and her son, Andrew Cameron-Walter.

Skiing on a Budget. Copyright © 1996 by Claire Walter. Printed and bound in the United States of America. All rights reserved. No part of this book may be reproduced in any form or by any electronic or mechanical means including information storage and retrieval systems without permission in writing from the publisher, except by a reviewer, who may quote brief passages in a review. Published by Betterway Books, an imprint of F&W Publications, Inc., 1507 Dana Avenue, Cincinnati, Ohio 45207. (800) 289-0963. First edition.

Portions of this text have appeared in *Skiing* magazine in different form.

Other fine Betterway Books are available from your local bookstore or direct from the publisher.

00 99 98 97 96   5 4 3 2 1

Library of Congress Cataloging-in-Publication Data

Walter, Claire.
    Skiing on a budget / by Claire Walter.
        p.   cm.
    Includes index.
    ISBN 1-55870-403-5 (alk. paper)
    1. 1. Skis and skiing—United States. 2. Deals—United States. 3. Family recreation—United States. I. Title.
GV854.4.W34   1996
796.93'0973—dc20   96-7628
                                                                              CIP

Edited by Cristine Antolik
Cover design by Brian Roeth
Cover photography by John Terence Turner/FPG International Corp.

TABLE OF CONTENTS

INTRODUCTION

Skiing has a reputation as an expensive sport. It certainly can be, but it also offers built-in opportunities for savings. Because the ski industry is seasonal and vulnerable, providers of skiing goods and services are so anxious to get new participants into the sport, move equipment and fill beds and lifts at off-peak times, that good deals abound. Some general strategies for being an economy-minded skier fit everyone. Other more specific advice applies to skiers in a particular geographic locale, age or interest group.

You *can* keep skiing from being a budget-buster. The common denominator of all the money-saving practices that you'll find in this book is the trade-off. To save money, you might trade more expensive, convenient-to-the-slopes lodging for a less costly, more distant one. You may trade this year's hottest fashions for gear or clothing that's slightly dated. You may trade a big resort for a smaller ski area. You may trade skiing during popular holidays for off-peak periods. If you keep alert to special values—sales, if you will—as they come along, you can save even more.

Many of us who are in love with the sport are willing to pay the price, and this book demonstrates that the price needn't be high. Others look at skiing as an investment in a lifetime of winter pleasure and outdoor activity with family and friends. Children as young as three start sliding down snowy slopes, and retirees with time to pursue their interests are heading for the hills in unprecedented numbers.

This book is designed to help you find ways to get in more skiing for your dollars. Where the advice is broad-stroke like buying a season pass (and buying it early), skiing in January when rates dip, taking advantage of airfare wars and so on, I just point to a general strategy. Where the advice is more specific and involves particular places, I've included specifics that are harder to find. Therefore, I'll guide you to ski areas with liberal teen-skiing prices, kids-free programs, budget dorms and the like. In some cases, such as ski-area birthday bashes and other once-a-season celebrations, I've given some examples of the kinds of values out there in ski-land. In other cases, like discount ski cards, I've listed every one I could find.

The main caveat of this book is that policies can change from one winter to another as ski-area ownership or management, weather patterns or the national economy change. I've tried to include ongoing promotions and eliminate one-season wonders. In the few places where I have given specific prices, they are to be taken as an example, not as a specific figure that will never change. The programs and policies specified here are based on those in effect during the 1994-95 ski season, double-checked during the editing process, which took place just before the 1995-96 season. Some may be gone by the time you read this, and some new ones may have appeared on the scene, so always check. A list of toll-free numbers and other resources follows in the appendix.

Use this book as a guideline, not as gospel—and have fun on the slopes.

Claire Walter
Boulder, Colorado
September 1995

CHAPTER ONE

GETTING STARTED

Whether you're a reluctant debutante, an enthusiastic novice or an accomplished skier looking for ways to introduce a newcomer to the sport, remember that learning to ski (and learning to ski better) can turn winter from a season to loathe to a season to love. The matchless beauty of snow-covered mountains, the satisfaction of learning a new sport and ultimately the thrill of skiing are captivating. Starting right is a smart investment. It's false economy to have a well-meaning friend "teach" you to ski. Pros know how to teach beginners, and cheap or even free learn-to-ski programs make those early skiing days hassle-free and economical. Don't stop taking ski classes once you've learned the rudiments. If you invest a few dollars in taking lessons now and then, you'll reap dividends. You'll enjoy mastering increasingly challenging terrain and gain more stamina. This translates into the ability to cover more (and more varied) terrain and therefore to wring more value for your dollar every time you ski.

LEARN-TO-SKI PACKAGES

At no time in your life will good deals be as abundant as during your first days on skis. Since the ski industry wants to seduce you and every nonskier, well-priced and even free introduction-to-skiing packages abound. The typical beginner package includes rental equipment, beginner instruction and a ticket for the lifts accessing the easiest slopes. The best packages are typically offered between the start of the ski season and Christmas. In some cases, the first day is even free. Many ski areas also give participants a coupon or some other incentive to return and continue skiing. For instance, as a "graduation present" after the first, low-cost ski day, Diamond Peak, Nevada, offers more than one hundred dollars of savings incentives for future visits. New Hampshire's Alpine and Nordic areas mount a free learn-to-ski week in mid-December, which actually includes beginner packages for new downhill skiers, snowboarders and cross-country skiers. The ski areas of Pennsylvania's Pocono Mountains run a similar program—Pennsylvania Learn to Ski Free Day—on a Friday in January. The Camelback Ski Area additionally offers free beginner packages on Tuesdays from early January through mid-March in their Introduce a Friend to Skiing promotion. Hunter Mountain, New York, has a similarly named Bring a Friend Skiing program, which gives a 50 percent midweek discount to any skier who introduces someone to the sport via a beginner lift/lesson/rental package.

START WITH MORE THAN ONE DAY

In the old days, many people launched their skiing careers by taking a ski week—five consecutive weekdays of lifts and lessons, usually one in the morning and one in the afternoon. Even without today's efficient lifts and user-friendly ski equipment, most people became reasonably competent in five days and, in fact, became hooked on the sport. Beginners can still sign up for full-week programs or plug into well-priced ski weeks promoted at several areas (see "Stretching Your Ski-Vacation Dollar," page 60). But recognizing that people today are pressed for time, a few ski areas encourage new skiers to invest more than one day but less than five to their first turns. Alpine Meadows, California's New Skier Club, starts folks with three days of lifts, group lessons and rentals. Monarch, Colorado, offers an inexpensive learn-to-ski package that includes lodging as well as a lift, lesson and rental package. Ninety-year-old Gray Rocks, Quebec, combines the charm of a French country inn with decades of offering some of the best learn-to-ski terrain and instruction you'll find. All-inclusive ski-week packages include twenty-two hours of ski instruction, which is ample for getting beginners off on the right ski. During all but peak holiday weeks, packages also include free ski rentals for beginners.

INNOVATIONS

SilverCreek, Colorado, is in a class by itself when it comes to beginners. This tiny resort, in the orbit of giant Winter Park, has carved a niche for itself as an ideal learn-to-ski and family area. With ample tame teaching and practicing terrain, a moving carpet to ferry skiers up the slope, a special women's-only learn-to-ski program and, most of all, modest prices, SilverCreek is a low-cost, low-priced place to start skiing. Perhaps partly as a response to its neighbor's example, Winter Park developed a twenty-acre sheltered beginner area called Discovery Park, with its own slow chairlift, warming hut and restrooms.

Sunday River, Maine, developed a new approach to ski instruction called the Perfect Turn, which is suitable for all levels from beginners to competition-level racers and freestylers. Traditional "instruction" has been replaced by "learning" in seventy-five-minute clinics that begin with what the skier is doing right and building on those strengths. This positive approach spawned the Learn-to-Ski in One Day guarantee, which invites new skiers who cannot ski independently to repeat their level-one program or get a full refund. The Perfect Turn has been franchised to several other areas, including its sister resorts of Attitash/Bear Peak and Cranmore, as well as Jiminy Peak, Massachusetts; Mt. Bachelor, Oregon; Ski Rio, New Mexico; and Blue Mountain, Ontario.

LEARN TO SKI, GUARANTEED

Other areas are so confident of their ability to launch beginners, and help experienced skiers improve, that they even offer guarantees. Aspen offers a guarantee to beginning skiers and snowboarders at two of the resort's ski areas. The Three-Day Guaranteed Learn to Ski is a lift-lesson-rental deal that promises a fourth day of instruction free to anyone who can't make it down a novice trail from the top of Buttermilk or from the Two Creeks quad chairlift at Snowmass at the end of three days. Elsewhere in Colorado, Crested Butte's QuickStart consists of one-and-a-half days of beginner lessons and two days' lift tickets. Anyone who cannot do wedge turns from the green-circle runs off the Keystone lift after the second day can choose either more instruction or a full refund. A novice who cannot ski from the top of Steamboat's Preview beginner chair "in a controlled manner" after a beginner lesson may repeat the class free. And SilverCreek issues a full refund to any new skier who cannot handle the Milestone beginner slope in a day. Angel Fire, New Mexico, guarantees that adults will be able to ride the beginner lift and do linked wedge turns at the end of their first day or they may continue taking lessons until they can do so, and that children six and older can ride the chairlifts and ski the mountain top to bottom after a week of lessons.

You can find guarantees at Eastern mountains too. The six-pack of resorts now under joint management that market themselves as the Peaks of Excitement, introduced an unconditional lesson guarantee for the 1995-96 ski season. Any skier or snowboarder at Maine's Sugarloaf/USA, New Hampshire's Waterville Valley or Vermont's Bromley, Killington or Mt. Snow/Haystack who is dissatisfied with a lesson at any level gets a voucher for an additional lesson, no questions asked. On its 1-2-3 Learn to Ski Program (named after the first three class levels) Loon Mountain, New

Hampshire, guarantees satisfaction or they'll give you a voucher for a free lesson. Further, Loon includes juniors from age six up in this guarantee, whereas most ski schools only make such offers to adults. Holiday Valley, New York, gives a complimentary lesson to beginners who do not learn the basics of skiing or snowboarding or experienced sliders who do not improve. And Hunter Mountain, New York, allows anyone whose skiing or snowboarding skills do not improve from lesson to lesson to take another at no charge.

New Hampshire has a dynamite statewide Intro to Skiing program that runs for an entire week in mid-December. In the Midwest, Michigan ski areas offer low-cost beginner lessons in Alpine skiing, snowboarding and cross-country skiing and give "graduates" of the first-day lesson discount coupons for equipment purchases. The idea seems to be that the commitment and enthusiasm to buy equipment is a built-in guarantee of a successful and satisfying beginner experience.

"FREE" IS THE BEST DEAL OF ALL

Only one thing beats low-cost skiing—skiing for free. If you can escape to Crested Butte during its Ski Free periods (see "Ticket Tactics," page 10), you can get free beginner lessons as well as free lift tickets, the two significant components of the resort's too-good-to-be-true offer. The lessons are set up as teaching stations that are staffed by instructors ready to help new skiers with the basics. As soon as you have the fundamentals of one skill, you move on to the next station and learn a new one. You can keep progressing steadily or retreat and practice on another portion of the slope until you're ready for the next step. In the East, Greek Peak, New York, also starts new skiers and snowboarders at free teaching stations. Jay Peak, Vermont, offers free lessons midweek in January and early February to guests staying at the Hotel Jay or on-site condominiums.

The four New England ski areas owned by LBO Enterprises—Attitash/Bear Peak, New Hampshire; Cranmore, New Hampshire; Sugarbush, Vermont; and Sunday River, Maine—offer complimentary beginner programs in their patented Perfect Turn system (see above). LBO's areas provide free intro-to-skiing and intro-to-snowboarding morning clinics to anyone over the age of seven on a first-come, first-served basis during nonholiday periods in December and January. Participants use complimentary rental equipment, including state-of-the-art parabolic skis from Elan in the ski program, and have the opportunity to continue at a substantial discount in the afternoon.

Other areas offer conventional-format instruction on a complimentary basis or with the addition of other incentives. Winter Park, Colorado, designates January as Learn to Ski Month and underscores it by providing beginners who purchase a full-day lift ticket with a free beginner ski or snowboard lesson. Diagonally across the state, Purgatory, Colorado, gives a free half-day skiing or snowboarding lesson to any first-timer thirteen or older with the purchase of a lift ticket. Ski Apache, New Mexico, flips it around and gives a free lift ticket to anyone who purchases a beginner lesson. Whitetail, Pennsylvania, has a bargain beginner package every Monday and gives a free lift ticket to any skier who brings a beginner to the area. While most areas only provide free instruction to "never-evers," which is the ski industry term for someone who has never ever skied, Ski Windham, New York, extends free lessons to low intermediate skiers. Waterville Valley, New Hampshire, has free first-time ski and snowboard lessons, rental equipment and lower-mountain lifts from just after Thanksgiving until shortly before Christmas. Eighteen New Hampshire ski areas cooperate in offering a free one-day beginner package for skiers or snowboarders in mid-December, the most comprehensive statewide offer in the country. Seniors can also take complimentary learn-to-ski instruction in late January. Other states from Pennsylvania to Oregon have had aggressive learn-to-ski promotions with free beginner packages and all sorts of extras. If your state or one near you has such a deal, urge your friends to come along and give the wonderful sport of skiing a try.

FREE TIPS AND TOURS

Sometimes you can get free pointers just by showing up at a designated place and time. Okemo, Vermont, has a complimentary ski tips station at the top of its Sachem quad chairlift. Skiers can take a run with an instructor who will give complimentary technique tips; these micro-lessons are given twice daily on weekends. Greek Peak, New York, stations instructors at the bottoms of Chairs 1 and 3 to take a run with guests and give free pointers; the resort also offers free two-hour clinics for ladies on Tuesdays, seniors on Wednesdays and men on Thursdays. If you want to be video-taped and get some pointers from Aspen's pros, meet instructors any day except Saturday at the No Problem Cabin at Buttermilk. Instructors from the Vail, Beaver Creek and Arrowhead ski-school corps give free tips daily at 11 A.M. At Heavenly Ski Resort, California/Nevada, Chevy Quicks are billed as a tune-up run with an instructor. The cost is just ten dollars, and it can help solve a small problem or two. The legendary powder-meister Junior Bounous has a complimentary program called Junior's Seniors for skiers sixty-two and older. He guides his group around Snowbird for two hours every Tuesday morning and offers inspiration, encouragement and tips for skiers whose reflexes, eyesight and go-for-it attitude might have diminished with the years.

Not ski lessons (and not conducted by ski instructors but rather by "hosts"), a meet-the-mountain tour is nevertheless a great investment in terms of time. If you're new to a ski area, especially a complicated one, it's an excellent way to get the lay of the land. Meeting times and places are generally posted at information desks, ski-school areas and the spots where these groups assemble. Some areas offer them daily; others only early in the week. Among the numerous areas offering complimentary tours are all four of the Aspen areas; Alpine Meadows, California; Loveland, Colorado; Purgatory, Colorado; Snowbird, Utah; Vail, Colorado; and Lake Louise, Alberta. Beaver Creek, Colorado's complimentary mountain tours have a social component. "Over-30 Singles" tours are on Mondays, environmental tours on Wednesdays, and "Before '44" tours for older skiers on Thursdays. At some ski areas, U.S. Forest Service rangers or volunteers lead complimentary interpretive tours focusing on the natural environment, including geology, plants and wildlife. Two resorts combine the best of both approaches. Billy Kidd, 1964 Olympic medalist and 1970 world champion, invites skiers to join him for a run from the Thunderhead Lodge at Steamboat, Colorado, any day he's in town. He offers pointers, mountain orientation and warm encouragement to skiers who follow in his wake. Nancy Greene, 1967 and 1968 World Cup winner and double Olympic medalist, does the same at Sun Peaks, British Columbia.

BEYOND THE BUNNY SLOPE

Budget-consciousness doesn't always mean *not* spending money. Often it means a wise investment in suitable new equipment or in further ski instruction to get the most out of skiing. If time allows, a true ski week is a far better investment than a series of weekends to improve your skiing. At destination resorts, especially in the West, a week will reap dividends in both skill level and sheer vacation enjoyment. Although it may not qualify as a budget vacation, you'll get your money's worth in terms of enjoyment and improvement. By contrast, nonholiday midweeks at East, Far West and Midwest ski areas are usually a time to snare bargain packages. The mountains are uncrowded and so are ski classes. In addition, you'll get five or more days of skiing for one round-trip from home compared with two or three on a normal weekend.

Though most skiers tend to eschew ski school once they are comfortable on blue runs, the best investment of all for many skiers is a specialty ski week aimed at those who want to break out of the ranks of the perpetual intermediate skier as well as really advanced skiers seeking to become even better. Courses focusing on racing, mogul skiing, powder or even extreme skiing can turn good skiers into great ones. And women who might not relate well to a male instructor or macho classmates often thrive in the women's workshops that now proliferate.

Private lessons are expensive, but sometimes the one-on-one attention by a gifted instructor is enough to overcome a real hurdle in your ski technique. In contrast with group lessons, which generally are one-and-one-half to two hours long, privates are generally blocked in one-hour increments. Some resorts give skiers an incentive to book a private. Alpine Meadows, for instance, knocks ten dollars off the private lesson price if you pick the 9 to 10 A.M. slot. In 1994-95, this discounted a one-hour private lesson to forty-five dollars per hour for one or two people. When you compare that to Alpine's two-hour group lesson at forty dollars per person, an early-bird private comes across as a good deal for sixty minutes of an instructor's undivided attention. Elsewhere, private lessons range from twenty-five to thirty dollars per hour at small ski areas in the East and Midwest to roughly forty-five to seventy dollars per hour at large destination resorts in New England and the West.

While most people sign up for lessons because they genuinely want to improve their skiing, others like the liftline-cutting privileges that ski classes enjoy. Especially at crowded holiday times, you might be willing to pay extra not to stand in line, and you're willing to consider that anything you learn on top of that to be a real bonus.

CHAPTER TWO

TICKET TACTICS

P eople pay particular attention to price points. For airline travel, the price point is the lowest airfare between two cities, even if that fare is seriously restricted and only available with limited-time advance purchase. In skiing, it's just the opposite. People tend to obsess about the highest price that one can possibly pay to ski. For instance, the most expensive single-day, at-the-window, adult lift ticket in 1995-96 was fifty-two dollars at Aspen and Snowmass, Colorado. During the same season, the average daily lift ticket across the United States remained around thirty dollars, but people never seem to talk about that.

Snaring a lot of low-cost tickets often doesn't require much effort. Ski areas routinely float their very best deals for skiing at the beginning and end of the season. Since early snow conditions may be marginal, many areas don't charge full freight for a mountain that is not completely skiable. When snow falls early, those bargain tickets buy the best skiing of the season. After Easter, when conditions are usually ideal and the weather is benign, skiers are bored, so areas again lower ticket rates (and sometimes also lengthen the skiing day). The definition of spring skiing, and therefore the lowered prices, vary by region. In the Middle Atlantic and Midwest, it can be as early as March, while in the West's high mountain ranges, spring skiing can be in April and later.

Beyond this simple matter of timing, you can adopt tactics to pare your lift-ticket costs to the absolute minimum. Obviously, price breaks depend on each individual ski area's policies, which can change from season to season, so the offers that follow are not written in stone. Rather, this chapter gives you an insight into the kinds of economies that have been out there in recent seasons. Even if you aren't skiing any of the areas listed here, these examples should give you an idea of what to look for whenever and wherever you ski.

JUST SHOW UP AT THE SHOW

Autumn means foliage, Halloween and ski shows. Scheduled across the continent, stretching roughly from early October through mid-November, these traditional ski-season previews can reap big benefits once the snow falls. The shows are platforms for hard- and soft-sell marketing by ski areas and other businesses that wish to reach skiers, but they also offer oodles of giveaways including posters, a chance to meet celebrity skiers, nuts-and-bolts news on the upcoming season and terrific entertainment, all in a carnival atmosphere. At several shows in key cities, including Denver, every attendee receives a one-day lift ticket to a nearby ski area. Ski discount cards, season passes and even vacation packages are booked and/or sold at these shows, and most are connected with a ski swap and/or a ski sale put on by a local retailer. You might even get lucky and win a ski vacation, a season pass or a couple of lift tickets.

Other events involving or promoting skiing sometimes offer coupons for free or discounted lift tickets. Concentrated in fall, when people are getting excited about the coming ski season, these events include showings of ski films and big sales run by major sporting goods stores or ski retailers (see "Gearing Up," page 36). You'll pay a modest admission charge when a ski film by Warren Miller or one of the other name producers comes to town, just as you'd pay for any movie, but entry to sales are free. Ski shops welcome all sorts of add-on values to draw customers to the sale—and hopefully encourage them to buy.

GET CARDED
NATIONAL CARDS

Among the staples at consumer ski shows, as well as at preseason sales at ski shops and other venues where skiers gather in fall, are salespeople hawking "ski cards." By presenting these plastic credit card-sized rectangles at participating ski areas, you'll get free or reduced lift tickets, as well as discounts on lodging, meals, car rentals and even airline travel. Some cards come with a fat directory detailing lift ticket deals, travel benefits and deep-discount days or even ski weeks. Others include an add-on such as a free hat or T-shirt.

Generally, the earlier in the season you buy the card, the less expensive it will be. The least expensive card bought in late summer or early fall can be as little as ten dollars. The most expensive card bought when snow is already on the ground might cost as much as sixty dollars. Also, if you buy more than one card for your household, you often enjoy savings on each card.

The major nationwide companies are:

CARD	BENEFITS
Ski Card International P.O. Box 3369 Evergreen, CO 80437 (800) 333-2SKI, (303) 670-2453	Maximum 200,000 cards sold annually, free ski days; discounts and special events at more than 150 ski areas; frequent-skier benefits at selected areas; travel, lodging and dining discounts in the U.S. and Canada; discounts anytime but Christmas
United States Recreational Ski Association	Not-for-profit organization that issues discount cards to its members; see "The Group" (page 119)
Universal Ski Ticket P.O. Box 578 Merrimack, NH 03054 (800) 653-5200, (617) 229-2589	Designed as a corporate gift or incentive program, the card is valid for skiing at scores of areas nationally; since it is not a discount program, it can be exchanged for unrestricted, full-price lift tickets
U.S. Ski Team Passport 1101 West Mineral Avenue Littleton, CO 80120 (800) SKI-TEAM, (303) 730-6226	Ticket price breaks at 250 resorts (some 35 exclusive to this card), plus discounts at more than 500 lodging properties and restaurants; discounts on car rentals and Northwest Airline tickets
World Ski Card P.O. Box 480825 Denver, CO 80248 (800) 525-7669, (303) 629-7669	Free ski days and discounted lift tickets; discounts at shops, restaurants, accommodations, travel suppliers; valid at 1,000 to 1,200 ski areas and other businesses

Be aware that newer card companies and those with ownership and management changes have been the subject of numerous consumer complaints from skiers who ordered but never received their cards. Be careful when selecting your plan. If you decide to sign up, pay by credit card—and scrupulously keep all documentation of the transaction.

REGIONAL AND LOCAL CARDS

National cards operate as independent businesses. Participating ski areas and other enterprises view them as part of their marketing programs to lure new customers. Localized discount cards are designed to induce frequent skiers to ski at the same area(s). Such cards, and their most recent prices, include:

CARD	BENEFITS
BC Ski Card	Purchase adult, youth or child's card at participating ski area (Cypress Bowl, Mt. Washington, Red Mountain, Silver Star or Whistler Mountain, BC) and receive 1 day of free skiing plus 10 to 25 percent discounts on subsequent lift tickets; price varies depending on where card is purchased; cards also available at selected sports shops
Gems of Colorado	Purchase $10 card before January 31 at one of the participating areas; ski once at each area for $10 on specific dates and up to four times for $22; $10 child's ticket available with each adult's ticket; valid at Arapahoe Basin, Arrowhead, Cuchara Valley, Eldora, Loveland, Monarch, SilverCreek, Ski Cooper and Ski Sunlight; details may change in future years
Ski The Catskills Lift-Off Card	Purchase a card for $11-$15, depending on quantity and date of purchase, and get one half-price ticket at each of nine New York State ski areas
Ski Three	Purchase a $15 card and ski free at each area on one designated day and get $5 off subsequent lift tickets (with some dates restricted at Angel Fire, Red River, and Taos Ski Valley, New Mexico)

Ski areas (or groups of ski areas under the same ownership) often issue their own discount cards, either for a nominal fee or even free for the asking. Look for cards for sale directly from the ski area(s), at fall ski shows, at regional ski shops and sometimes even at gas stations that also sell lift tickets during the ski season. As with season passes and national cards, some ski-area cards are cheaper if bought before a specific date. Others cost less for additional people in the household, and others are available for adults, juniors and seniors at different prices. Many are not valid or restricted during major holiday periods. Excellent programs abound and reward loyalists with terrific values for skiing frequently. They are ideal for skiers who don't hit the slopes quite enough to make a season pass worthwhile.

Some such programs charge a modest fee in exchange for season-long discounts, but these pay off quickly. Colorado is the card capital. Vail and

Beaver Creek's economical Colorado Card is good for a free early-season day, plus daily lift-ticket discounts throughout the winter. You also save time because your discounted day is automatically charged to your credit card, sparing a stop at the ticket window. Purgatory's Flex Pass is valid for discounts on daily lift tickets. Loveland, which traditionally is early to open and late to close, offers the Loveland Pass, which provides particularly long-running benefits for early- and late-season skiing. The card gives the normal daily lift-ticket discounts and every fifth day free, too. The Sunlight Savings Card for individuals and the Business Club Savings Cards for enterprises with ten to twenty-five employees produce good weekend savings on lift tickets and even better ones during nonholiday midweeks.

Bear Mountain, California's FrequenSKI is a low-cost program awarding one point for each ten dollar expenditure. A certain number of points can be redeemed for free lift tickets, and members get additional discounts for food, ski school and rentals. Up in the Tahoe area, Ski Homewood's economical Frequent Flier provides a five dollar discount on each one-day lift ticket. It pays for itself after three days of skiing, and every fifth day is free. Nearby Sugar Bowl's low-cost Frequent Skier Program nets five dollars off four days' lift tickets with the fifth day free. Kirkwood, California's Avid Skiers Card nets one free day of skiing for every four lift tickets purchased.

Mammoth Mountain, California, has a multitiered deal that enables you to choose various options based on the cost and your perception of how much you'll use the benefits. The Mammoth Club has three levels of membership good for various discounts on lift tickets, lodging, dining, retail purchases, ski waxing, lessons, race clinics and miscellaneous specials. Snow Summit, California, calls its frequent-skier program the Gotta Ski Team. "Members" save on every day-and-night lift ticket during the season. It also includes coupons for savings on lessons, rentals and food. Greek Peak's Greek Peak Club also has different levels. All members ski midweek and evenings for 50 percent off; weekend day tickets are 25 to 40 percent off, depending on the level. Elsewhere in New York State, Ski Windham's Frequent Skier Card offers discounts every day of the season, including Christmas week. Nearby Hunter Mountain, New York, charged twenty-five dollars for the Frequent Skier Card it inaugurated for the 1995-96 ski season. The first use netted a four dollar discount off the lift ticket, and the discount for every use thereafter provided an additional one dollar to a maximum of fourteen dollars. After as few as three uses, Stratton, Vermont's Frequent Skier Card pays for itself with various savings on lift tickets every day except holidays. The Bolton VIP Card nets 40 to 50 percent off each lift ticket at that mid-sized Vermont mountain.

Other areas' cards are free, especially in places like Colorado, where competition is fierce. Neighboring Breckenridge, Keystone and Arapahoe Basin, under joint ownership, issue one of the best cards. Their Ski 3 Card provides discounts on lifts, lessons, meals, rental equipment, lodging and other services. There is also one free skiing day before Christmas. A time-saving bonus is that day skiing is charged directly to a pre-approved credit card. Nearby Copper Mountain, Colorado, a long-time partner in the Ski The Summit joint marketing efforts, now issues its own free card. The Copper Card discounts lift tickets, lessons, rental equipment, meals and lodging all season. The Monarch VIP Card offers a lift-ticket discount at this high-altitude powder haven. Ski Rio, New Mexico's Powder Hound Club offers a free "starter day" early in the season and discounts on lift tickets, ski school, ski shop and other activities such as dogsled and snow-mobile tours throughout the season.

Some cards reap bargain rates and special services. Steamboat's free STM (for Save the Most) Card is valid for lift, lodging and ski-school discounts, as well as an on-demand fax information line and exclusive snow-conditions forecasts. With each two-day or longer lift ticket purchase, a child twelve and under skis free. Winter Park's Powder Plus low-cost program brings significant discounts on daily lift tickets and also charges them automatically to a preapproved credit card, enabling participants to avoid a stop at the ticket window. In addition, there's free skiing every seventh day; plus free ski accessories and savings on transportation, dining, lodging and other services. Vail and the Keystone/Breckenridge/Arapahoe Basin family developed similar auto-charge programs that save time as well as money.

Kirkwood, California's Avid Skier Program is good for one free day of skiing after each four days of paid skiing. At Loon Mountain, New Hampshire, you get a free midweek lift ticket after five days of skiing, or you can eat your way to free skiing. Loon's Frequent Eater Club, introduced in 1995-96, credits a set dollar amount of food and nonalcoholic beverages at breakfast and lunch toward a free nonholiday midweek lift ticket. At Okemo, Vermont, and Wildcat, New Hampshire, you earn a free day after paying for seven.

Snowbasin, Utah, sells a very low-cost Discount Card good for dollars off daily lift tickets. Stratton Mountain, Vermont's low-cost Frequent Skier Card reaps various discounts for early- and late-season, midweek and week-end skiing (except during holiday peaks). By these measures, the cards issued by Telluride, Colorado, and Jackson Hole, Wyoming, are fairly costly, but they carry hefty lift-ticket discounts at these two powerful peaks. The low-cost Skier's Plus Card (cheapest when purchased before December 15) provides five dollars off an all-day ticket at Sandia Peak and Ski Santa Fe, New Mexico, except during the Christmas-New Year's holidays.

Cards valid at more than one mountain are rarer in the East, but with an escalation of mergers and consolidations among ski resorts, may become more common. The Edge Card, one of the rare free cards in New England, is good for discounted and free lift tickets at Sunday River, Maine; Attitash/ Bear Peak and Cranmore, New Hampshire; and Sugarbush, Vermont. The Peaks of Excitement Card gives a free day after six days at Bromley, Killington, Mt. Snow or Haystack, Vermont; Sugarloaf, Maine; and Waterville Valley, New Hampshire. A Visa card option rewards skiers with points every time they use the card, and the points are redeemable for ski-related products and services. Ski Liberty and Ski Roundtop, Pennsylvania, issue their Frequent Skier Card, good for substantial discounts off day or night skiing. The Empire Ski Card, which must be purchased before January 1, is good for lift ticket discounts at New York state-owned Gore Mountain and Whiteface Mountain any day but Saturday and also includes one free day.

The bottom line is that most of these cards pay for themselves after just one or two uses. In many cases, they aren't the *only* way to reap discounts, but they are convenient. Some skiers join several programs and keep all the cards in the car or boot bag. Skiers who habitually use these cards save oodles over the course of the season.

SAVE BIG WITH A SEASON PASS

If you ski a lot, nothing beats a season pass for absolute value. Not only is your cost per skiing day cut way down, but you can save still more by signing up early. At most areas, the earlier you buy your pass, the cheaper it will be. Multitier pricing abounds, with passes incrementally more expensive until the ski season kicks off. Most areas charge a certain fee for the first adult in a household, with increased savings for each additional family member, and many areas that offer only children's and adults' day tickets, issue family season passes or teen and/or student passes to encourage teenage skiers and snowboarders to hit slopes.

When deciding whether to invest in a pass or to opt for one of the other frequent-skier inducements, a little math and an honest assessment of your skiing patterns are useful. Divide the cost of the pass by the price of a single-day ticket to determine what your break-even day is. If you truly plan to ski at that one area more than the break-even point, it's a good deal. If you live close to the area and have a season pass, you'll be more likely to give yourself the bonus of popping over to the mountain for a few hours. After all, you've already paid for a season's worth of sliding.

Variations on the season pass abound. Season pass holders at any of the IntraWest ski areas (Stratton, Silver Creek and Snowshoe in the United States, and Blackcomb, Panorama and Tremblant in Canada) are eligible for half-price skiing at all the company's other mountains. Belleayre, Gore Mountain, Hunter Mountain and Whiteface Mountain, all in New York, sell inexpensive nonholiday midweek season passes. Pass holders at Holiday Valley, New York, receive lift-ticket discounts at nearby Catamount, Hunter Mountain, Plattekill and Windham. Big Sky, Montana, similarly invites season pass holders from other Montana areas to ski all day for the price of a half-day ticket. Jackson Hole, Taos Ski Valley and Montana ski-area season pass holders get a full day of skiing at the half-day rate at Michigan's Boyne Resorts. Season pass holders at Welch Village, Minnesota, ski free at Grand Targhee, Wyoming, all season long. Brundage, Idaho, offers a very low-cost grandparent add-on to a conventional family season pass. Okemo, Vermont, provides outstanding season pass values for skiers sixty-five and older. In 1994-95, the fifty dollar limited pass was valid every day except Saturdays and holidays, and the one hundred fifty dollar unlimited pass was good every day of the season.

Some traditional late-skiing areas such as Mammoth Mountain, California, and Killington, Vermont, offer late-season passes for spring and summer skiing. In exceptional late-snow years, these can be unbeatable values. In 1995, the Arapahoe Basin-Breckenridge-Keystone complex sold a bargain season pass ($199 for adults, $99 dollars for children) good from May 1 until the lifts closed. At A-Basin, that wasn't until the second week of August!

PRE-PURCHASE A LIFT TICKET FOR BIG SAVINGS

In highly competitive markets such as Colorado and Utah, locals (and savvy visitors) reap savings by buying their lift tickets before they get near the slopes. Ski retail and rental shops, gas stations and even supermarkets sell discounted lift tickets. Local chambers of commerce, as well as hotels and local and out-of-state ski shops, sell discounted tickets. Ski Sunlight's version is called the Ten Day Picture Pass, which looks like a season pass but works like a voucher. You show it to get a lift ticket any ten days during the ski season. Skiers get five dollars off their lift tickets to Kirkwood, California, when they purchase them at Bass Ticket Outlets in northern California and northern Nevada, as well as discounts on ski school and children's programs. Some areas, like Wintergreen, Virginia, also sell tickets at MWR locations (military installations' Morale, Welfare and Recreation offices). You can also economize by buying a book of lift tickets or lift-ticket vouchers. These little treasures are typically issued in ten- and twenty-day denominations for both adults and children. Do keep in mind that when you purchase the actual lift ticket instead of a voucher or coupon that must be redeemed at the mountain, you get in more skiing time because you bypass the ticket window.

TICKET VOUCHER BOOKS DELIVER SKI VALUES

Coupon or voucher books, available directly from ski areas or from their representatives at fall ski shows, are good for a preset number of skiing days and represent excellent values to those who ski often but not enough to justify a season pass. Some must be purchased before a specific date. When you want to ski, you turn in a coupon for a day ticket.

SKI AREA	THE DEAL
Alpine Meadows, CA	10-coupon book, with leftovers usable the following season
Boyne Resorts, MI	Tik Pak, 10-ticket coupon book
Brighton, UT	5- and 10-coupon book
Brundage, ID	15-ticket book for midweek and weekend savings
Hunter Mountain, NY	5- and 10-day packs priced for adults, students and children
Killington, VT; Mt. Snow/Haystack, VT; Sugarloaf, ME; Waterville Valley, NH	Skier's Dozen Ticket Booklet, 12 coupons redeemable at any participating area, including holidays; bonus coupon for free day of early- or late-season skiing; phone special number, (800) 88-PEAKS, to purchase
Massanutten, VA	Various-length versions for midweek and night skiing
Mt. Bachelor, OR	Mini-season pass, good for 10 days of skiing
Park City, UT	Utah Resident Coupon Book, available only to in-staters in 5- and 10-ticket versions
Snowbird, UT	Pre-purchase 15 individual tickets, 20 to 40 transferable family tickets and/or 5 or more ski-school classes before December 15 for savings

Solitude, UT	5- and 10-coupon book
Steamboat, CO	Super Club members have option of purchasing 10-ticket book
Sundance, UT	10-ticket voucher book (additional fee required for use on Saturdays and selected holidays)
Whitetail, PA	Sixer, savings for advantage purchase of 6 nights of skiing

BIRTHDAY BASHES

Ski areas celebrating landmark birthdays often roll back lift tickets (and sometimes other prices) to those offered on opening day. Keep an eye out in local media, where such promotions are generally announced. Badger Pass, California, perhaps had the best deal of all, a free season pass to skiers who shared their fortieth year with the ski area. Donner Ski Ranch, California, sells ultracheap tickets and rentals during their annual Anniversary Week during the last week of January. Ski Windham, New York, celebrates its founding with heavily discounted lift tickets every year on the Tuesday following Martin Luther King, Jr.'s Birthday.

The birthday isn't always the ski area's. On Pulaski Day (March 6), Indianhead Mountain, Michigan, traditionally gives a free lift to anyone who is surnamed Pulaski, is a graduate of any Pulaski School or is a resident of the town of Pulaski. Loon Mountain has traditionally provided bearded skiers who show up on the real Lincoln's Birthday, February 12, with a free lift ticket. Cannon Mountain, New Hampshire, knocks one dollar off the lift ticket for every green item of clothing worn on March 17, which may or may not be St. Patrick's real birthday.

Some theme discounts actually have nothing to do with anyone's birthday. Belleayre, New York, for instance, offers discounted lift tickets (as well as free beginner lessons and free NASTAR racing) to residents of various New York counties on specific dates in January. Mt. Snow, Vermont, has offered half-price Valentine's Day lift tickets to anyone submitting a unique ending to the "Roses are Red, Violets are Blue" ditty.

SKI FREE

In 1991, Crested Butte, Colorado, launched Ski Free—no-strings-attached free skiing—roughly between Thanksgiving and Christmas. Because the resort was all staffed up with lift operators, patrollers, ski instructors, snowmaking and grooming crews, food service personnel and other employees needed to keep a ski area, management figured they might as well bring

skiers to town to eat, sleep, party and shop in the slack time between
Thanksgiving and Christmas. The dates have varied somewhat from year
to year, but the no-strings policy remains: free skiing at designated times,
with no minimum number of days, requirement to stay in a participating
lodge (except over Thanksgiving weekend, in 1995 anyway), or any other
restrictions. In 1996, Crested Butte also introduced a spring version of Ski
Free in April, an offer that may or may not continue.

With record numbers of skiers at the Butte during Ski Free, other resorts
naturally have been motivated to make a similar offer. With a minimum
of four nights of participating properties in Park City, Utah, skiing is free
at the Park City Ski Area from the mid-November scheduled opening
through mid-December. Keystone, Colorado, gives free skiing at Keystone,
Breckenridge and Arapahoe Basin with at least one night's lodging at Keystone from season's opening, which is normally in October, through the
middle of December. Diamond Peak, Nevada, offers free skiing on four
consecutive days in December as part of its Northern Lights Celebration.
Other resorts tie free skiing in to overnights at selected properties. These
include Telluride, Colorado, both early and late in the season; Ski Rio,
New Mexico, during the post-Thanksgiving, pre-Christmas period, again
from early January through early February and again at the very end of
March; Holiday Valley, New York, from opening until just before Christmas for guests at The Inn; Whiteface, New York, before Christmas to
guests at participating lodges in Wilmington and Lake Placid; Jay Peak,
Vermont, for early- and late-season guests of the Hotel Jay or resort condominiums and free midweek lessons in January and early February; and
Northstar-at-Tahoe, California, for resort guests on two-night or longer
packages. Lodging guests at Bolton Valley, Vermont, and Shawnee, Pennsylvania, ski free at those mountains. Guests at Vermont's opulent Woodstock Inn ski free at nearby Suicide Six any day except Saturday. Midweek,
nonholiday lift tickets at King Pine, New Hampshire, are free for guests
of the nearby Purity Springs Resort, while those staying at the Hanover
Inn ski free at Dartmouth Skiway. It is often possible to buy discounted lift
tickets through lodging properties, even if there is no free skiing attached to
sleeping there. Usually, such offers are stated in the literature or posted,
so be alert.

GUARANTEES MINIMIZE MONETARY RISK

If you hate a movie and walk out after it's started, or if you can't get into
the book you've bought, you've bought the ticket or the tome before you
realize you don't like it. But a number of ski areas are more generous.

Some are so confident of their conditions and facilities that they have instituted some sort of guarantee program. When conditions are questionable or if you just like to try before you buy—or at least get a refund or credit should you decide not to stay and ski—programs like these cut the risk of shelling out the bucks:

SKI AREA	GUARANTEE
Bear Mountain, CA	Return ticket within 1 hour of purchase for a credit voucher good another day later in the season
Boyne Highlands, Boyne Mountain, MI	Return ticket within an hour of purchase for a credit voucher toward another day
Diamond Peak, NV	Return ticket within 1 hour of purchase for a credit voucher good another day later in the season
Greek Peak, NY	Return ticket within one-half hour of purchase for credit voucher good for another lift ticket
Gunstock, NH	Return ticket within 1 hour and 15 minutes of purchase for full, no-questions-asked refund
Holiday Valley, NY	During early season, guests get a full refund on 2-day or longer packages unless at least 3 of the 12 lifts are running
Hoodoo Ski Area, OR	Lifts open at 9 A.M., but attendants do not begin checking lift tickets until 10 A.M.
Indianhead, MI	Return ticket within an hour of purchase for credit voucher good for another day of skiing
Killington, VT	Return ticket within 45 minutes of lift opening for credit toward another day of skiing within 12 months
Lake Louise, AB	10 Minute Guarantee, full refund if the wait at one of the three base-area lifts is more than 10 minutes
Loon Mountain, NH	Unconditional Conditions Guarantee, return lift ticket before 11 A.M. in exchange for voucher good for another day's skiing; rental equipment and unused lesson also can be "returned"
Okemo, VT	First half-hour of every day is free, so you can try before you buy

The Pass*, WA	Single Ride Quality Test ticket, low-cost 1-ride ticket or return regular ticket within 1 hour of purchase for voucher for a future lift ticket
Pico, VT	Happy Skier Guarantee, return lift ticket within half-an-hour and receive a voucher for use later in the season
Schweitzer Mountain, ID	Return ticket within 1 hour of purchase for a voucher good for another day
Silver Mountain, ID	Voucher for the value of a lift ticket returned within an hour of purchase
Ski Windham, NY	Snow Check, voucher for the full value of a lift ticket returned within 1 hour of purchase, valid for another day of skiing
Squaw Valley, CA	No Waiting in Line policy carries a full refund to skiers who wait in liftlines more than 10 minutes
Whitetail, PA	Whitetail's Wonderful Warranty, voucher for another day's skiing if you are dissatisfied and return your ticket within 1 hour of purchase
Wildcat, NH	Wildcat Ski Guarantee, voucher for the full value of a lift ticket returned before 10:30 A.M. nets a ticket of equal value

*Alpental-Snoqualmie-Ski Acres-Hyak

LOW PRICE FOR LIMITED LIFTS

Savings incentives for beginner lifts or sometimes for older and/or slower lifts are sprinkled in ski country. Even some of America's really significant resorts have a value deal of that sort. Perhaps the most attractive plans are tiered pricing for adults and children. Winter Park, Colorado's Mini-Mountain Ticket is valid on six of the area's twenty lifts, and there's also an ultracheap ticket good only on the Galloping Goose beginner lift. Nub's Nob, Michigan, took another tactic—replacing a tow with a low and slow beginner chair, which is free. Mighty Snowbird, Utah, offers three ticket options. The most expensive ticket is good for all lifts including the tram, a less expensive ticket is valid for all chairlifts, and a low-priced beginner ticket is only for the Chickadee chairlift. Sugarloaf, Maine, has a unique pay-by-ability scale. The Mid-Mountain Ticket is good on four chairlifts, sixteen novice and intermediate trails, and 1,500 feet of vertical. The really inexpensive Mini-Mountain ticket accesses three lifts and more than two miles of gentle novice runs. Sun Valley sells budget tickets good only on the novice paradise called Dollar Mountain, the resort's beginner hill.

FEWER DOLLARS FOR FEWER LIFTS

SKI AREA	THE DEAL
Alta, UT	Beginner area lift ticket at savings
Alyeska, AK	Free skiing on 2 chairlifts for ages 5 and under
Attitash, NH	Discount ticket for novice lifts
Brundage, ID	Low-cost ticket for 2 beginner lifts
Copper Mountain, CO	Free low-season and late-season use of beginner chairlifts
Hunter Mountain, NY	Reduced-cost lift ticket for Hunter One beginner area
Jackson Hole, WY	Chairlifts-only single- and multi-day tickets a few dollars less than all-lifts versions, which include tram
Killington, VT	Children 6 and under ski free on Snowshed beginner lifts with paying adult
Nub's Nob, MI	Free use of beginner chairlift
Okemo, VT	Free use of beginner Pomalifts
Mt. Bachelor, OR	Midway Special, half-price ticket for lower lifts
Mt. Hood Meadows, OR	Free use of beginner tow
The Pass*, WA	Beginner chairlift ticket at savings; ultra-low-cost rope tow ticket
Schweitzer Mountain, ID	Low-cost ticket for beginner lift
Silver Mountain, ID	Economical ticket for beginner chairlift
Snowbird, UT	Chairlift-only ticket less than all-lifts ticket that includes tram; also, bargain ticket valid only for Chickadee beginner chair
Steamboat, CO	Low-priced ticket for Headwall and Southface beginner lifts
Sugarloaf, ME	Pay-by-ability policy (see above for details)

Sun Peaks, BC	Low-priced ticket for Sundance Ridge novice area, including high-speed quad chairlift
Sun Valley, ID	Bargain tickets for Dollar Mountain, the beginner/novice complex
Taos Ski Valley, NM	Less than half of regular day ticket price for novice lifts only; free with purchase of Yellowbird learn-to-ski package
Wildcat, NH	Free use of beginner chairlift and 3 beginner slopes
Winter Park, CO	Mini-Mountain ticket for six lifts and 210 acres; additional super-cheap ticket only for Galloping Goose beginner lift
Wolf Creek, CO	Low-cost lift ticket for beginner chairlift

* Alpental-Snoqualmie-Ski Acres-Hyak

PAY AS YOU SKI

Technology has made customized skiing possible. In systems such as Ski-Data, new-age lift tickets and even wristwatch-like devices are encoded for a season, a week or a day of skiing—or a point system for skiing by the run or by the hour. Under a point system, each lift is allotted a certain point value, which is deducted when the skier moves through a turnstile at the bottom of the lift. The approach is especially economical for those who don't ski enough to make a season pass worthwhile but live close enough to the lifts for a few hours of skiing here and there. Among the early users of such systems are Attitash, New Hampshire; Big Sky, Montana; Loon Mountain, New Hampshire; Mont Ste.-Anne, Quebec; Mt. Bachelor, Oregon; Northstar-at-Tahoe, California; and Solitude, Utah. Mt. Bachelor and Solitude's plans are so flexible that they are transferable. Also, Snow Valley, California, and Mont Orford, Quebec, offer skiing by the hour. Caberfae and Crystal Mountain, both in Michigan, do pay-as-you-ski the simple, old-fashioned way—selling two- and four-hour tickets, which are especially popular with skiers from nearby communities. Greek Peak, New York, has a five-hour ticket valid any time. Loveland, Colorado's four-hour mid-day ticket combines half-day pricing with a way to avoid both the morning and evening rush hours on Interstate 70.

HALF-DAY TICKETS: BARGAIN OR NOT?

When you look at the typical ski area rate sheet, a half-day lift ticket usually is good for fewer than half of the hours when the lifts are running but costs substantially more than half of a full-day ticket. It doesn't take an Einstein to figure out that this is not a particularly good value. However, half a day's skiing is better than none, and time is a factor. Try to get your money's worth by showing up immediately at the start of the half-day (usually 12:30 or 1:00 P.M.), and try to get in as many runs as possible while full-day patrons are lingering over lunch, and ski till closing time. For really late arrivals, Hunter Mountain, New York, has an unusual low-cost late-day ticket that doesn't start until 2:45 P.M. If you can't start skiing until afternoon, it's worth looking into twilight tickets, which often are less expensive than all-day skiing and bridge the time from afternoon to night skiing. If you are weekend skiing and want to get a homebound head start on Sunday, take advantage of the morning half-day offer many areas now provide. If you return your all-day ticket before a certain specified time, you'll get a refund to the half-day rate.

NIGHTTIME'S THE RIGHT TIME TO SAVE

Night skiing takes place in a special focused world of bright snow, eerie shadows and blackness beyond. During a snowstorm, it takes on a particular surrealistic cast. But night skiing can also be a bargain. At The Big Mountain, Montana, for instance, it is about one-third the cost of a day ticket and yet offers a respectable twelve runs, four lifts and maximum vertical of 1,100. Ski areas near metropolitan areas are the night-skiing capitals and may be as busy after dark as during the day (and perhaps busier than during nonholiday midweeks). Ski Paoli Peaks, Indiana, a small banana-belt ski area whose major market is Louisville, Kentucky, puts on a dozen nights of Midnight Madness every winter, with skiing from midnight to 6 A.M. Night skiing there can be fun, but it's usually not the bargain it is at destination resorts. A combined ticket for both day and night skiing may be the most economical of all. If you've got the stamina, the Super Skier ticket enables you to ski The Pass from 9:00 A.M. to 10:30 P.M. for just a few dollars more than a day or twilight ticket alone.

LIGHTS ON FOR SAVINGS

SKI AREA	THE DEAL
Belleayre, NY	Fantastic Fridays, full- or half-day lift ticket includes night skiing during January, February and March

Bintz Apple Mountain, MI	Ticket valid 10 A.M. to 10 P.M.
Bogus Basin, ID	Budget ticket valid from 5 P.M. to 10 P.M.
Bretton Woods, NH	Economical twilight ticket from 2 P.M. to 10 P.M.
Donner Ski Ranch, CA	Low-priced full- or half-day ticket valid for evening skiing Wednesday through Sunday, plus holidays
Gunstock, NH	2 for $20 Tuesdays, nonholidays, offers ultra-low-cost night-skiing ticket
Keystone, CO	Any ticket (full-day, multiday or afternoon) good for night skiing until 9 P.M.
The Pass*, WA	Family Nights, youngsters to age 17 pay half-price on Saturdays; limit 2 children per adult
Ski Liberty, Ski Roundtop, PA	Flexticket, available for any 4- or 8-hour period during the day or evening
Schweitzer Mountain, ID	Night ticket starts at 3 P.M.
Squaw Valley USA, CA	Economical afternoon-night ticket
Temple Mountain, NH	Day ticket also good for skiing until 10 P.M. nightly
Timberline, WV	All regular-season multiday tickets valid for night skiing
Whitetail, PA	Bargain evening add-on to day ticket
Wintergreen, VA	Free night skiing (and free rental equipment) with purchase of multiday lift ticket; a single-day ticket may be upgraded for twilight and night skiing for $5

Alpental-Snoqualmie-Ski Acres-Hyak

MIDWEEK DEALS

Except during holidays or at major destination resorts far from population centers, weekday skiing generally is a good value because the absence of crowds means you'll get maximum runs for your skiing dollar with minimal downtime while you're waiting in liftlines. Some areas even do better, either with special rates or with add-on values, that make a few hours of skiing cheaper than going to a movie.

PROMOTIONAL TIE-INS

Radio stations, newspapers and peddlers of products from milk to beer often target the skiing market, which is perceived to be well-heeled, with

WEEKDAYS ARE SAVINGS DAYS

SKI AREA	THE DEAL
Belleayre, NY	Every Monday is Couples Day, with 2 adults skiing for one moderate price including free nursery care for preskiers; also third day (either Friday or Monday) is free with weekend stay at participating lodge (reservation required)
Bolton Valley, VT	Vermonter Days, discounted midweek lift ticket to in-state residents with valid ID
Bousquet, MA	Free rental of ski or snowboard package with purchase of a nonholiday midweek lift ticket
Bretton Woods, NH	Tuesday Ladies' Day, 2-for-1 Wednesdays and Thursday Men's Day discounts; $10 off all-day Monday or Friday lift ticket for season pass holders from any other ski area
Bromley, VT	Midweek ticket less than half of weekend and holiday rate
Butternut Basin, MA	Nominally priced ski lesson with purchase of lift ticket on Monday or Wednesday
Cannon Mountain, NH	Every Tuesday is 2-for-1 day
Donner Ski Ranch, CA	Midweek skiing at little as half the weekend price; ultra-low-priced night skiing
Grand Geneva, WI	2-for-1 on Mondays, Ladies' Day on Tuesdays, Men's Day on Wednesdays and Company Day on Thursdays, with bargain lift, lesson and rental packages and optional lunch
Gunstock, NH	Bargain "2-for" lift tickets on Mondays and Tuesdays
Haystack, VT	Back to the 'Stack, free weekday of skiing after 6 nonholiday midweek days
Homewood, CA	Wild Wednesdays, with 2-for-1 lift tickets
King Pine, NH	Free group lesson with full-day lift ticket for women on Wednesdays and men on Thursdays; 2-for Tuesdays for both day and night skiing

Kirkwood, CA	Low-cost midweek season pass
Mont Ste.-Marie, QU	Every Tuesday is two-for-one day
Mt. Rose, NV	2-for Tuesdays
Mt. Sunapee, NH	Every Tuesday is 2-for-1 day
Okemo, VT	Super Seven Frequent Skier Program; card good for a free day of skiing after 7 nonholiday midweek days
The Pass*, WA	Bargain midweek lift tickets, especially low-cost Mondays and Tuesdays
Ragged Mountain, NH	Bargain midweek lift tickets
Saddleback, ME	Bargain midweek lift tickets, except holiday weeks
Ski Homewood, CA	Wild Wednesdays, 2-for-1 lift tickets after New Year's
Ski Windham, NY	S.N.O.W. Card (Ski Now On Weekdays), 1 free day of skiing after 4 full-priced non-holiday weekdays
Sugarloaf, ME	White World Ski Week, generally the last week in January, with ultra-low-cost day tickets
Whitetail, PA	Bargain day and night lift tickets for men on Mondays, women on Tuesdays and seniors (50 and older) on Wednesdays
Wildcat, NH	2-for-the-price-of-1 skiing every Wednesday
Wintergreen, VA	Wednesday Family Days, youngsters 17 and under ski free when accompanying an adult throughout the season except Christmas week

* Alpental-Snoqualmie-Ski Acres-Hyak

a variety of special offers, especially during the early season or January. The discount may involve clipping a coupon from a newspaper or presenting a candy wrapper or soda bottle cap. For example, buying the "Discovering Utah" multimedia CD-ROM netted a booklet of vouchers good for two-for-one and discounted lift tickets at areas all over the state, and Hertz offered a voucher for one free lift ticket at Park City or Deer Valley with a winter rental from Salt Lake City. Crested Butte's "interactive tour manual," also a CD-ROM, came with a coupon for a free lift ticket to that Colorado resort. Snickers Discount Days gave ten dollars off on lift tickets at Copper Mountain, Colorado, each Sunday in January. A Quiz Kidz Meal at participating Quizno's Subs in Colorado netted a coupon for a free children's ticket at Steamboat. At Holiday Valley, New York, skiers enjoyed two-for-one night-skiing three evenings a week in conjunction with the local McDonald's. Donner Ski Ranch, California, jointly promoted with various northern California ski and snowboard shops to bring lift ticket prices down to as little as one dollar—yes, one dollar!

Skiers who brought Oberto products to Snoqualmie, Washington, skied free. Coupons on Pepsi products purchased at a Rosauer Supermarket in the Pacific Northwest were good for a discount on a Silver Mountain, Idaho, lift ticket and bottle hangtags printed with a sweepstakes entry form with prizes ranging from dinner at a resort restaurant to a ski vacation at Silver Mountain and the nearby Couer d'Alene Resort. The beverage company also prints discount tickets to New Mexico ski areas on twelve-pack wraps and cups distributed in New Mexico and west Texas. Coupons on 7-Up products were good for discounted lift tickets at Gore Mountain, New York, with part of the proceeds donated to the Muscular Dystrophy Association. An L.L. Bean Premier Pass, valid for a free half-day group lesson and two days of ski rentals, was provided at selected areas with the purchase of certain winter products. Such promotions are subject to cancellation or change, but this roundup gives you an idea of the kinds of specials to look for.

SKIING AND DOING GOOD

Ski savings and good deeds often go hand in hand. Many ski areas host benefit races, but these are not always bargains. However, you can make a charitable donation or be a good environmental citizen while saving money. In addition, you can reap ski benefits by volunteering your time on the slopes (see "Work to Ski," page 128).

SKI FOR CHARITY

Ski areas, such as New Hampshire-owned Cannon Mountain and Mt. Sunapee, often donate season passes and lift tickets to fund-raising auctions for public radio and television, which traditionally are bid on at 50 to 70 percent of the ticket price. The American Lung Association has sold a coupon book good for discounted lift tickets at various California, Nevada and Utah ski areas.

Sometimes, the deal is more direct. Steamboat opens its ski season with Scholarship Day—and a fifteen dollar lift ticket—with proceeds going to the Steamboat Springs Winter Sports Club Scholarship Fund. Skiers who donate a plaything to Ski Homewood, California's annual toy drive, held on a mid-December weekday, ski for five dollars. A donation of canned food for the needy nets five dollars off a day ticket at Stowe, Vermont, in early December, a fifteen dollar opening-weekend ticket at Sugarloaf, Maine, or a free opening-day ticket at Angel Fire, New Mexico. Proceeds of neighboring Ski Rio's annual Nickel A Pound lift ticket on opening day go to the New Mexico Museum of Natural History. The math is simple: body weight times five, so that a 150-pounder can ski or snowboard all day for $7.50. Hunter Mountain, New York, donates revenues from the Friday after Thanksgiving to the National Ski Patrol System. Even if the skiing's not a bargain, it's for the benefit of a very good ski organization.

BE AN ECO-SKIER

Obviously, the more people you pack into a car, the cheaper the per-person transportation becomes. Specific savings may change, but recent rewards for the environmentally conscious have included incentives to cut down on driving. Carpool with at least three friends or relatives, and Ski Santa Fe, New Mexico, will give you five dollars off one lift ticket. Wedge five people into the car and Brighton, Utah, lobs two dollars off everyone's lift ticket. Take a TART (that's for Tahoe Area Regional Transit) bus to Ski Homewood and that resort offers a one dollar discount, which skyrockets to five dollars during Christmas-New Year's, Martin Luther King, Jr. Weekend and President's Weekend peaks. A Heavenly Valley lift-ticket voucher purchased at northern California Safeway stores includes a five dollar discount when you enter from the California side or nine dollars off when starting your ski day at the less congested Nevada side. Whether or not the ski area rewards you financially for carpooling, if you divide the cost of gas or the parking fee, if there is one, by the number of the skiers in the vehicle, you can't help but save.

GEOGRAPH-SKI

Ski areas sometimes run special promotions for folks from various states (see "Stretching Your Ski-Vacation Dollar," page 60, for vacation programs), which are occasionally offered for day skiing. At Stratton, Vermont, in-state residents ski for very little (fifteen dollars during the 1995-96 season) on four specific days during the season, and residents of Connecticut, Massachusetts, New Hampshire, New Jersey, New York and Rhode

Island are invited to enjoy the slopes for ten dollars more on other assigned days. At the end of the season, Stratton thanks everyone with another fifteen dollar day. Saddleback, Maine, has special vacation weeks for skiers from New Brunswick and Nova Scotia, while Crested Butte puts on Flat-landers Ski Week in early December, in conjunction with its Ski Free program, when mid-country ski areas might not yet be open.

SKI BY AGE

Many ski areas offer free skiing to youngsters to age five or six and to seniors seventy years and older, but free or discounted skiing for older children (usually up to age twelve or thirteen) or younger seniors (age fifty-five to seventy) are harder to come by. If you or a member of your family falls into either age bracket, comparison shopping can save you dollars. A perusal of *The White Book of Ski Areas*, an authoritative statistical guide, indicates some of the best deals at both large and small ski areas, but direct inquiries to places you want to ski will alert you to any changes in pricing structure and policies. A selection of programs for children and teens is also listed in the "Family Values" chapter (page 48). Competition spurs on favorable pricing. Where one ski areas institutes an especially fine value for children or seniors, the chances are good that some of its neighbors will match them.

STUDENT SAVINGS

Some ski areas make a special effort to reach local youngsters, such as Winter Park's Monday Madness, which provides ten days of low-cost ski-ing to students in Colorado's Grand County school system, which is on a four-day week. In addition to the more common school-sponsored ski outings and racing or freestyle teams, youngsters may be rewarded for good grades, a pledge to remain drug- or alcohol-free or for simply living nearby. Wildcat, New Hampshire, sells a really inexpensive after-school children's ticket (and offers bargain lessons) and also makes a specially priced multi-visit ticket available to local youngsters enrolled in the D.A.R.E. and S.A.D.D. programs.

In addition to low-cost tickets, which in fact may be called student rates, some ski areas offer additional discounts to college students—with a valid ID. The Extra Credit Card is one of the most appealing offers for eastern college students. This low-cost, interchangeable card offers dis-counted midweek (and frequently weekend) skiing at Bromley, Haystack, Killington and Mt. Snow, Vermont; Sugarloaf, Maine; and Waterville

Valley, New Hampshire; for new skiers, it can also be used for a lift/lesson/ beginner lift ticket package.

College identification isn't the only way to get a discount. Those who have chosen military service will find that several areas, including Stratton, Vermont; Whitetail, Pennsylvania; Wintergreen, Virginia; and The Pass, Washington, offer discounts to skiers with a military ID.

SKI AREA	THE DEAL
Ascutney Mountain Resort, VT	Midweek college students' rates
Attitash, NH	Midweek discount for college students
Belleayre, NY	College students and faculty may buy economical midweek lift tickets
Bousquet, MA	Low-cost lift tickets any time
Bromley, VT	Extra Credit Card, valid for discount skiing with college ID, daily except Saturday
Cannon, Loon and Gunstock, NH	College Value Season Pass, interchangeable pass valid daily except Saturdays during non-holiday periods
Gore Mountain and Whiteface, NY	Student Ski Card, allowing full-time students to ski any day of the season for discount
Greek Peak, NY	College students with ID ski for 50 percent off any midweek day or 25 percent off any weekend or evening
Haystack, VT	Extra Credit Card, valid for discount skiing with college ID, daily except Saturday
Hunter Mountain, NY	College students to age 18 (with ID) may ski at teen rate
Killington, VT	Extra Credit Card, valid for discount skiing with college ID, daily except Saturday
Mt. Snow, VT	Extra Credit Card, valid for discount skiing with college ID, daily except Saturday
Okemo, VT	Half-price all-day lift ticket, nonholiday midweeks
Perfect North Slopes, IN	Holiday Season Pass, for college students at home during Christmas break
Shawnee Peak, ME	Discount for students with college ID
Silver Mountain, ID	Discount for students with college ID

Ski Windham, NY	Midweek discounts with college ID
Stowe and Sugarbush, VT	The Big Pass, good all season at both areas, available to registered full-time students
Sugarloaf, ME	Extra Credit Card, valid for daily discount skiing with college ID
Waterville Valley, NH	Extra Credit Card, valid for discount skiing with college ID, daily except Saturday
Windham, NY	Discounted student lift tickets, including special Sunday rate
Wintergreen, VA	Low-cost lift tickets on Tuesdays and Thursdays from January to the end of the season

VALUE SKIING FOR SENIORS

"We grow too soon old und too late schmart," goes an old Pennsylvania Dutch slogan. Older skiers can be the smartest skiers by picking resorts that offer exceptional deals for seniors. "Senior" is a pretty loose term. If you're looking at California's Big Air Green Valley Snowboard Park, it means anyone over thirty-five. The park gives a free lift to anyone who brings an oldster of thirty-five or more to ride. On ski programs, fifty or fifty-five is about as young as a senior gets to be. Inspired by the 70+ Ski Club, which lobbied on behalf of skiers who are "up there," many ski areas now offer free skiing for septuagenarians and older.

BEST DEALS FOR SENIORS   Most ski areas offer special rates for seniors sixty-five and older, and many offer free skiing to those seventy and older. Those with even more appealing deals include:

UNITED STATES

SKI AREA	THE DEAL
Angel Fire Resort, NM	Free skiing for age 65 and over
Balsams Wilderness, NH	Senior rates begin at age 55
The Big Mountain, MT	Senior rates begin at age 62
Bousquet, MA	Free skiing for age 65 and over
Burke Mountain, VT	Senior rates begin at age 60; Senior Skier Tuneup is a special, low-cost workshop
Cascade Mountain, WI	Senior rates begin at age 55
Cataloochie Ski Area, NC	Free skiing for age 65 and over

Chestnut Mountain, IL	Ultra-low-cost night ticket for age 55 and over
Copper Mountain, CO	Over The Hill Gang with special ski days and discounts for age 50 and over; geared to residents of the Denver-Boulder area
Crested Butte, CO	Half-price skiing for ages 65 to 69
Crystal Ridge, WI	Free skiing for age 65 and over
Dodge Ridge, CA	Free skiing for age 62 and over
Hoodoo Ski Area, OR	Free skiing for age 65 and over
Jackson Hole, WY	Half-price skiing for age 65 and over
Jay Peak, VT	$5 lift ticket for age 65 and over; Silver Peaks Club, Tuesday workshop for age 50 and over
Kirkwood, CA	Silver Streaks, free clinics for seniors every nonholiday Wednesday; senior rates begin at age 60
Loon Mountain, NH	Flying 50s Plus, meets twice a week and includes continental breakfast, guided skiing and skills development
Middlebury College Snow Bowl, VT	Age 62 and over pay student rate
Okemo, VT	Ultra-low-cost season pass options for age 65 and over; half-price ski lessons
Park City, UT	Less than half-price skiing for ages 65 to 69
Pico, VT	Tenth Mountain Division veterans ski free
Scotch Valley, NY	Half-price skiing for ages 50 to 70
Ski Apache, NM	Economical season pass for age 62 and over
Ski Cooper, CO	1 Senior Day per month with bargain skiing for age 50 and over
Ski Rio, NM	Free skiing for age 65 and over
Ski Sundown, IA	Senior rates begin at age 55
Ski Sunrise, CA	Free skiing for age 65 and over
Ski Windham, NY	Half-price midweek skiing for age 65 and over
Snowbird, UT	Discounted skiing for age 62 and over
Snow Canyon, NM	Free skiing for age 62 and over
Squaw Valley USA, CA	Ultra-low-cost ticket for age 65 and over

Steamboat, CO	Discounted lift tickets for ages 65 to 69
Stratton, VT	Senior rate begins at age 62
Sundance, UT	Free skiing for age 65 and over
Sunrise Ski Resort, AZ	Ultra-low-cost day or night ticket for age 65 and over
Timberline, WV	Senior rate for skiers 60 and over
Waterville Valley, NH	Silver Streaks, a club for skiers 55 and older that meets every Wednesday for organized skiing, après-ski socializing, racing clinics and availability of discounted lodging
Whitetail, PA	Silver Streaks for age 50 and older every Wednesday

CANADA

SKI AREA	**THE DEAL**
Bromont, QU	Senior rates begin at age 55
Canada Olympic Park, AB	Senior rates begin at age 55
Le Relais, QU	Senior rates begin at age 55
Mont Garceau, QU	Ultra-low-cost skiing for age 60 and over

CHAPTER THREE

GEARING UP

Skiing is an incredibly equipment-intensive sport. You need such "hardware" as skis, bindings, boots and poles and such "soft-wear" as warm, water- and wind-resistant clothing, plus gloves or mittens, hats or headbands, insulating underwear and warm socks. Fortunately for skiers, rental equipment for beginners and advanced skiers abounds, and ski clothing can often be used for general winter wear. Because interest in skiing has been relatively flat, sales and bargains are common.

The nineties have been a time of great technological advances in equipment. Especially, revolutionary ski designs have penetrated deep into ski lines in a very short time. For example, cap skis, which started out as exclusive top-of-the-line at selected brands in the early nineties were available in midpriced and even package skis by the middle of the decade. The advent of other exciting new technologies—notably hourglass-shaped or parabolic skis for Alpine skiing and short and mid-length skis for cross-country—means that never-used traditional models, which are still quality items, have been coming on the market at unbelievable bargain prices. Look for them at ski sales.

Since ski gear is designed for active sports, it tends to stand up well. Experts say that well-maintained equipment *can* virtually last a lifetime for an average skier, and that even aggressive skiers can get a hundred days or more out of a pair of skis. Therefore, you can use equipment until your skill level increases and skiwear until it is hopelessly out of style, but you probably won't want to. Since you'll be probably upgrading every few years, it's wise to save money any time you can.

RENTAL EQUIPMENT FOR BEGINNERS

When you're first learning to ski, the basic lift-lesson-rental package is the best deal. It offers one-stop shopping for equipment you'll need to start skiing: a set of skis, boots and poles; a ski lesson or two; and a lift ticket, usually offered at an excellent price. Don't be discouraged, however, if the rental equipment doesn't feel as if it's really helping you make those first turns. Much gear designed for beginners is lowest-common-denominator equipment. It's meant for those first days on skis, but it does not provide an accurate impression of what more sophisticated ski gear can do. Entry-level boots are the golden mean, designed to provide a reasonably close fit to as many feet as possible, and beginner skis will let you glide, do a basic turn and stop. Still, not all rental operations are conscientious about caring for skis, and the ability of rental equipment to perform well at this basic level can be diminished with use. After you've spent a few days on skis, when bargain packages including rentals are less commonly available, you'll need to consider the benefits of continuing to rent versus acquiring your own equipment.

KEEP RENTING

If you only ski during an annual vacation, you'll probably want to continue to rent. To assure the equipment you want and, perhaps, get a package-like price break, reserve your equipment when you book your air, lodging, ski lessons and other vacation components. Most resort central reservations numbers, tour operators and travel agents can do that. If you are skiing above a novice level, pay a little extra for "performance" skis. Your investment will be rewarded by the dividend of more control and greater enjoyment. If you live close to the slopes but just ski occasionally, renting may still be right for you. Renting close to home might reap a price break, and some rental shops either take discount coupons (such as two-for-one rentals), give you a free day's rental after six, ten or twelve days, or both. Many in-town rental shops also allow you to pick up your equipment the evening before day one and return it the morning after your last day, which saves you time at the mountain and gives you more time to ski. On the other hand, if you rent at the ski area, you may pay a little more and dip into your skiing time, but you do have immediate recourse if you have boot fitting or other equipment problems.

The Peaks of Excitement ski resorts (Bromley, Killington, Mt. Snow/Haystack, Vermont; Sugarloaf/USA, Maine; and Waterville Valley, New Hampshire) have a convenient season-long rental program. After one visit to the rental shop, your records as to ski and boot size and model is accessible via computer at all the other areas, so the right equipment awaits you anytime you ski at any of those mountains. During the 1995-96 ski season, when this program was introduced, unlimited season-long rentals cost $125.

If you ski rarely, you can even consider renting clothing. Some ski shops in destination resorts (and even the rental shop at Salt Lake City Airport) have a supply on hand, often to help visitors whose luggage didn't arrive when they did, and other sunbelt areas like Ski Beech, North Carolina, rent clothing because many of their guests don't ski often.

PURCHASE A PACKAGE

Once you've fallen in love with skiing, you'll probably want the convenience and cachet of your own equipment. Ski shops answer novices' needs with "packages," an economical option that provides new skiers with serviceable components of what you'll need to ski: skis and bindings, often boots and sometimes poles. Snowboard packages include boards and bindings, and perhaps boots. When you buy a package, binding mounting and adjustment are usually included in the price. You won't be getting high-performance gear, but in the beginning, you won't need it, and when you're ready to trade up, you'll have a better idea of what you're seeking.

LEASE PROGRAMS

A compromise choice is the season-long lease option, which is not unlike automobile leasing, except that you lease skis by the season. You use the gear as you would your own, and since you return it after the snow melts, you don't have to store it over the summer. The following year, you can try another brand, ski length or model or get the same type of gear again. Leasing works for adults because it's a good value, especially for new skiers who like to be comfortable on their equipment, prefer not to hassle with rentals every time they ski, and because their skills improve. In any case, you get reasonably up-to-date equipment at a fraction of the cost of purchasing, and if, after several years of leasing, you ultimately decide to buy your own, you'll have test-skied several brands and models. If you like your leased equipment, you can usually arrange to buy it at the end of the season for far less than the retail price would have been. Late summer is a good time to select an equipment package. When it starts getting cold, ski shops get crowded and the selection narrows.

Leasing is especially good for children, who rarely can use anything for more than a winter. New Jersey's Ski Barn has the prototypical program: You buy your child's bindings and rent skis and boots. The bindings are checked, readjusted for your child's increasing body weight and skill level and remounted each season to fit his or her current boot size. Because youngsters also like to take friends skiing, Ski Barn throws in a free weekend rental with a season-long lease of children's equipment. Pedigree Ski Shop of Stamford, Connecticut, leases individual items as well as full packages. Denver's Eskimo Ski Shop offers a free equipment exchange to accommodate either children's growth or the need for upgraded equipment as they advance. The shop also has a rent-to-own policy with lease fee applicable for the purchase of equipment. Deke's Sporthaus in Campton, New Hampshire, has established a Boot Club with season-long leases on adults' and children's boots. White Mountain Ski & Sports in Great Neck, New York, throws in a midseason trade-in for youngsters who outgrow equipment before winter is over as well as a free tuning during the season. Occasionally, you come across a really unusual equipment offer. Big White, British Columbia, is so safety-conscious that it lends free helmets to young skiers and snowboarders on its slopes.

SHOP THE PRESEASON SALES

Whatever your needs or wants in the way of equipment or clothing, you can get great buys if you time your shopping well. Contrary to the image of skiing as an expensive sport, it is one of the few specialties where the best prices are available shortly *before* high season. September and October are the top months, comparable to bargains on Halloween costumes before October 31, Christmas ornaments between Thanksgiving and Christmas or shamrocks the first two weeks in March. Gigantic Gart Sports started the trend with Sniagrab, which is "bargains" spelled backward. The sale begins, as it has every year since 1954, on Labor Day Weekend at Garts' flagship store in Denver. Carryover merchandise from past season, manufacturers' excess inventory and special purchase ski equipment, clothing and accessories are marked with rock-bottom price tags. Sniagrab naturally launched a slew of imitators, not just in Colorado but all over the country. They are usually advertised in the local media with the zeal of car dealerships clearing out inventory. Even if you don't need new equipment, be sure to shop the sales for clothing or accessories you might want.

TRY BEFORE YOU BUY

Once you're ready to purchase performance equipment, it's wise to invest some time before you invest your money. If you can afford to buy only one equipment category, start with boots. Only three factors really count in deciding which is the right pair for you: fit, fit and fit. Go to a good ski shop, determine the price and performance level you need, and spend as much time as possible trying boots on. Listen to the counsel of an experienced salesperson and let him or her fit you. Then walk around, flex the boots, walk around some more, keep them on and walk around still more. This indoor try-on won't replicate what you'll experience on snow, but it will weed out boots that never will fit. Also consider such adjustments as custom insoles, extra padding and, especially for women, heel wedges to customize your boots. If your feet tend to get cold even in a well-fitted boot, consider investing in a heater. The cost may seem hefty, but you'll recoup it in runs that you *didn't* miss while you were indoors warming your toes.

Very few ski shops give customers the opportunity to test boots on the snow (the Colorado-based SportStalker chain, Kenny's Double Diamond Ski Shop in Vail and Danzeisen & Quigley in Cherry Hill, New Jersey, being notable exceptions), but many retailers offer demo skis. If you rent demos at your local ski shop, you'll have a whole day or weekend to decide whether you like them. If you test skis at a resort, you may have the opportunity to try several pairs for one fee. If you buy the skis, the charge is usually deducted from the purchase price. Pedigree Ski Shop's try-after-you-buy policy features a customer-pleasing Love 'Em or Leave 'Em guarantee, with a full refund if you don't love your new gear after you've skied on it.

A number of ski areas also host demo days, at which representatives of major equipment manufacturers allow skiers and snowboarders to try out equipment. Think of it like test-driving a car, except you'll probably have to plan on doing so sometime between Thanksgiving and the second week of December (or sometimes in early January and occasionally even February), and you have to pay to do so. Usually, you'll need to present a valid driver's license and pay a modest fee in addition to your lift ticket. Demos in the East traditionally include Attitash, New Hampshire; Big Boulder, Pennsylvania; Bromley, Vermont; Camelback, Pennsylvania; Jack Frost, Pennsylvania; Gore Mountain, New York; Hunter Mountain, New York; Loon Mountain, New Hampshire; Mt. Snow, Vermont; Ski Windham, New York; Stowe, Vermont; Sugarbush, Vermont; Sunday River, Maine; and Wintergreen, Virginia. Camelback, Pennsylvania, has a couple specific snowboard days in February. In the Midwest, Indianhead, Michigan; Mt. Brighton, Michigan; Wild Mountain, Minnesota; and Wilmot, Wisconsin, host annual demos. In the West, Bear Valley, California; Boreal, California; Keystone, Colorado; Kirkwood, California; Loveland, Colorado; Schweitzer Mountain, Idaho; Ski Santa Fe, New Mexico; and Snow Summit, California, usually schedule demo days. Ski Rio, New Mexico, puts on a demo program once a month. Stowe's ski school also offers unusual demo classes called Equipment Makeover for skiers ready to move up to a higher-performance level of equipment. These three-hour sessions include demo tryouts and guidance on what to look for. It's not inexpensive, but it's a lot cheaper than the wrong choice when you're ready to make a major investment. If you're considering buying Rossignol skis, ask your local Rossi dealer for a "test pass" to Rossignol test centers, which have been established at Vail, Killington, Mt. Snow, Sugarloaf and Blackcomb. They are operational all season long, and there is an additional summer center on Mt. Hood, Oregon. Dynastar's first test centers were established at Bear Mountain and Northstar-at-Tahoe, both in California, with more projected elsewhere. To demonstrate its belief in new ski design, the ski school at Purgatory, Colorado, includes the use of parabolic or hourglass-shaped skis in its Introduction to Parallel Workshops and fat skis in its Powder Morning Workshops.

CATALOG ORDERS REAP SAVINGS

Because so much of its population skis, the Rocky Mountain region is known as a competitive market, with unreal price wars throughout much of the year. One firm, Ski & Snowboard Gear Direct, extends these price breaks on adults' and children's equipment and clothing to customers around the country. Expect to pay 20 to 30 percent below suggested retail on current, in-line products and 30 to 90 percent off on closeouts from previous seasons. A limited supply of used demo equipment is also available. Generally, four brands of skis, two or three kinds of boots, eight snowboard makes, three or four snowboard boots, about five snowboard bindings and four or five brands each of ski and snowboard clothing are inventoried and appear in the company's catalogs, which can be ordered by calling (303) 494-4343 or writing to 1803 South Foothills Highway, Boulder, CO 80303. The firm also issues supplementary lists, which are faxed on request by calling (415) 598-4343.

Another order merchant, Sierra Trading Post, specializes in outdoor equipment and clothing, sold at 35 to 70 percent off manufacturers' suggested price. Their inventory is strongest in the kinds of crossover merchandise that is equally useful for winter hiking or biking and skiing, but it's worth sending for their catalog if you are in the market for ski jackets, longjohns, gloves, goggles or a hat. You can phone them at (307) 775-8000 or write to 5025 Campstool Road, Cheyenne, WY 82007. The best-known East Coast equivalent is Campmor, which is heavy into camping and backpacking gear, but also carries such ski-appropriate merchandise as jackets, pants, fleece tops, longjohns, turtlenecks, sunglasses and socks. Call (800) 230-2151 or write to P.O. Box 700-F, Saddle River, NJ 07458-0700.

BUY AT THE END OF THE SEASON

Retailers prefer not to carry inventory over the summer, especially for big-ticket skis, boots, bindings, snowboards and clothing that may not carry next season's color or graphics scheme. In urban areas, sales usually are in full swing by late February or early March, which may be just in time for your vacation. At resorts, sales kick in as season closing approaches. Many shops in ski resort towns have excellent deals on leftovers throughout the summer. Rental and demo equipment is frequently sold off at the end of the season, too. If snow conditions have been outstanding, ski bases are often in equally outstanding condition. If snow conditions have been marginal but business has nevertheless been good, examine the bottoms and edges carefully. If you live or travel near a skiwear or ski-equipment supplier, you can sometimes get exceptional buys on leftover inventory, samples and demos. Pre Skis in Salt Lake City and Spyder ski clothing in Boulder, Colorado, are among the companies with well-known warehouse sales.

BAG THE BONUS

If you must buy (or at least try) the newest gear or ski fashions, you might be eligible for a day of skiing as a bonus, or perhaps you can get new equipment as a bonus for a travel booking. Scour ads both in your local newspaper and in national skiing magazines and go through the mail for discount coupons for such extras. Few such value-added promotions last more than a season, but if you're shopping, be on the lookout for tie-in deals.

In recent years, for instance, if you bought a pair of K2 giant slalom racing skis in 1994-95, you received a certificate for a half-day ski lesson. In other years, you could get a free lift one-day ticket at your choice of three dozen ski areas across the country simply by trying on a pair of Dolomite boots and sending in a coupon. Clothing buyers could redeem the hangtag from a Sun Ice adult-size jacket or ski suit for a day of skiing at one of fifty areas or add a day to a multiday ticket at Aspen with the purchase of Obermeyer ski clothing. Perhaps the best bonus dates back to the 1989-90 season, when the purchase of a pair of Kästle skis reaped a "passport" good for a day of skiing at each of fifteen areas across the country.

Silver Mountain, Idaho, has had a series of tie-ins with ski companies, originally with K2 and later with Rossignol. In its most recent incarnation, purchasing a pair of Rossi V4K skis at a participating ski shop in the Northwest netted two days of skiing at Silver Mountain and two nights' lodging at the Coeur d'Alene Resort, while a four-day, five-night vacation package at the resort reaped a pair of skis. If you booked an Amtrak ski vacation by mid-December, your name was automatically entered in a sweepstakes, with top prizes of Dynastar skis. When Raichle introduced the Thermo Flex custom boot liner, the company supported it with a coupon in national publications good for thirty dollars toward selected boot models.

Even if you are not ready for a major equipment or clothing purchase, take advantage of the value-added coupons ski shops often use to build traffic. You may get additional free or discounted services, such as ski tuning or waxing.

CARE PROLONGS EQUIPMENT LIFE

If you want to get the best performance and longest wear from your equipment, and protect its ultimate trade-in value, take care of it—just as you change the oil in your car. If you want to safeguard equipment from corrosive road salt and sand, use a ski bag or at least binding covers when carrying gear on a rooftop tack. Proper ski and snowboard maintenance includes sharpening edges and filling in nicks and gouges in P-tex bottoms, and good sense means you'll have your bindings checked at least once a season. Unless you have the right equipment and skills, these measures are best left to a ski mechanic. Herman's, the powerhouse East Coast sporting goods chain, sells the inexpensive *Skiers' Service Coupon Book* for various discounted maintenance and tuning services, including tuneups, hot waxing and boot binding systems testing. However, if you want to start saving even more money on maintenance, it's easy to learn to wax your own skis. *Alpine Ski Maintenance and Repair* by Seth Masia (Contemporary Books, Chicago, IL), *Ski Tech's Guide to Maintenance and Repair* by the editors of *Ski Tech* (John Muir Publications, Santa Fe, NM) and *World Class Ski Tuning Manual* by Michael Howden (WCST Publishing, Portland, OR) tell you how to go about it.

Most specialty ski and snowboard shops carry at least a limited assortment of care and repair products. A comprehensive inventory, as well as the books above and tuning and fitting manuals, handbooks and videos, are available from Toolworks, P.O. Box 212, Mt. Shasta, CA 96067; (800) 926-1600 (phone orders and technical information) or (800) 926-9904 (fax orders).

KEEPING EQUIPMENT SAFE

Once you've invested in good equipment, don't tempt anyone else to take it. Especially at busy places and busy times, and extra-especially at ski areas with easy highway access, take preventive measures to make sure that your equipment remains yours. The traditional security measure is to separate your skis on the rack at the day lodge. The flaw is that an ambitious thief with an eye on your gear will watch where you put your skis, wait until you enter the building and make off with your equipment. A ski lock can be a good investment. Some areas, such as Eldora, Colorado; Heavenly, California; Hoodoo Ski Bowl, Oregon; Silver Mountain, Idaho; Snowmass, Colorado; Waterville Valley, New Hampshire; and Wintergreen, Virginia, offer free daytime ski checks.

RECYCLING SKI GEAR

You can recycle your equipment through a ski swap, an ad in the newspaper, a yard sale, a note on bulletin boards in ski and snowboard shops and sporting goods stores or a consignment shop, and you can find good deals on used equipment from those sources. If you're selling, keep your conscience clear and don't pass off dangerous old junk, even for a bargain price. If you're buying, be aware that others may not have your conscience. Ski bases might be irreparably damaged, bindings might not meet current releasability standards and boot soles may be so worn that bindings do not function properly with them. To get safe equipment at a good price, it's best to know something about skiing equipment—or take along a knowledgeable friend who believes in the better safe-than-sorry credo, and even then, have a ski technician look it over before you use it.

Any time you buy used equipment from any source other than a ski shop or a swap staffed by a certified ski technician who inspects for currency, it is a small but wise investment to take your purchase to a local ski shop to have the bindings adjusted to your boots and serviced. If the shop refuses to work on them because they are too old or otherwise not in good condition, believe the technician and invest in another pair. It is false economy to ski on outdated or unsafe bindings.

Some ski shops take used gear, either as trade-ins, buy-backs or on a consignment basis. On buy-backs customers will probably be credited with 50 percent of your outlay toward the next season's selection, so the following season's user gets an even better value since the gear is a year older and has a winter's mileage on it. Since dealers prefer not to devote valuable floor space to second-hand stuff, particularly as peak selling season approaches, prices tend to be extremely reasonable. This is especially true for children's equipment, which many retailers take as a customer service and to build loyalty. Any Mountain Sports in Cupertino, California; Boulder Ski Deals in Boulder, Colorado; Deke's Sporthaus in Campton, New

Hampshire; Outdoor Sports in Wilton, Connecticut; and Pedigree Ski Shop in White Plains, New York, do a fine trade-in business, with an emphasis on kids' gear, and Boston-based Ski Market's fifteen shops in New England cheerfully accept both adults' and children's gear. Mountain View Sports in Keystone, Colorado, does a brisk consignment trade. Just as you can buy used gear, you can trade in equipment when you're ready to upgrade—or when your children need another size.

A growing franchise called Play It Again Sports, as well as local consignment sporting goods stores, may have a good assortment of used and sometimes even new ski gear. Such stores are normally quite choosy about what they accept, so equipment is likely to be fairly current. Thrift shops in such ski towns as Aspen, Mammoth Lakes and Steamboat Springs often have great buys in ski clothing and gear, and even your local Salvation Army or Goodwill stores, hospital thrift shop or other sources for used items often have ski equipment too, but the same caveats as buying from private individuals apply.

Swaps are tried-and-true fund-raisers for urban and suburban ski clubs, school systems, children's museums and a myriad of other good causes. Normally held on just one or two weekend days in fall, ski swaps split proceeds between the seller and the cause. Equipment may be anything from new (or nearly so) to badly banged up, though most swaps insist that bindings and boots meet current safety standards—and have volunteer ski shop employees or other experts on hand to assure that they do. Not only is a swap a good place to pick up equipment and, often, clothing at 50 to 75 percent off retail, but you can make a few dollars by selling items you no longer use. If you sign up to work, you'll probably have time to look the goods over early, and some even offer volunteers first crack at purchasing before the doors are open to the public.

The Los Angeles Ski Club Council puts on a mammoth swap in conjunction with Skidazzle, the big consumer ski show in late November, and Denver's mid-October swap, with proceeds going to the National Ski Patrol System is reputedly the nation's largest. Two Washington cities boast great swaps—Seattle for the Crystal Mountain Ski Patrol in early November and Spokane for supporting the Mt. Spokane Ski Patrol at the end of October. Elsewhere, top swaps include the Down East Ski Club Swap in Portland, Maine, shortly after Thanksgiving, the swap on behalf of ski patrols at Montana Snowbowl and Marshall Ski Area in Missoula, and several large swaps in the greater Denver area for various good causes. In addition to those close to home, some of the best are held at ski areas or in ski resort towns. The biggest are those in Vail, Park City and Tahoe

City, with about fifteen to twenty thousand items for sale. So saddle up
the car, remember your checkbook, enjoy the fall foliage and head for the
swaps:

THE AREA OR RESORT TOWN	THE SWAP
Aspen, CO	Tailgate Sports Swap, benefiting the Aspen Valley Ski Club, held in mid-October
Belleayre, NY	Generally first weekend in October, swap plus season pass sales, children's program and fair with food, crafts and entertainment
Bousquet, MA	New and used equipment sale, benefiting the Bousquet Ski Club, in early October
Breckenridge, CO	Held annually in early October to benefit the Breckenridge Ski Club
Butternut Basin, MA	New and used equipment, plus new clothing and accessories, held the last weekend of September
Greek Peak, NY	Last weekend in October, to benefit Greek Peak Ski Club; includes closeout merchandise from about a dozen New York State and Pennsylvania ski shops
Holiday Mountain, NY	Last day of discounted season pass sales, normally in early October
North Conway, NH	For the Eastern Slope Ski Club, in early November
Okemo, VT	Held the weekend before Thanksgiving, benefiting Okemo Ski Patrol
Park City, UT	Benefiting the Park City Education Foundation, a weekend in early November
Smugglers' Notch, VT	Proceeds go to Smugglers' Junior Race Program, mid-October
Steamboat Springs, CO	Steamboat Winter Sports Club Swap benefit, weekend in early November
Stratton, VT	Stratton Mountain School Ski Sale, last weekend in November
Tahoe City, CA	Tahoe Community Nursery School, late October
Vail, CO	Ski Club Vail, huge swap held each October

DRESS FOR SUCCESS

When you're participating in winter sports, "success" does not mean making a fashion statement. Success means dressing appropriately to combat the elements. After all, if you're too cold to ski, your lift ticket time will be clicking away while you're thawing or drying out in the lodge. The secret to keeping warm is layering your clothing. Start with thermal underwear, top with water- and windproof ski pants and a warm wool or fleece sweater, add a windproof parka, jacket or anorak. A wool, blend or fleece hat, a neck gaiter if it's really cold and warm gloves or mittens complete the basic ski outfit.

Today's materials laugh at the weather. Fabrics and insulation materials designed to keep you warm and dry have become the industry norm. To save money, shop the sales as you would for ski equipment, and if you live far from a resort area, consider saving time with mail-order skiwear. Look for garments and accessories that will do double duty. A number of companies now make "cross-over" garments, which are suitable for the slopes and also for casual streetwear. A child's ski parka will double as a sturdy winter school jacket, but since quality ski gloves and mitts, which youngsters tend to lose, cost more than the regular back-to-school variety, it's best to keep the good stuff for the slopes.

Skiwear needs to be warm and weatherproof, so a careful reading of the hangtags will accurately tell you about the outer fabric, insulation and lining of each garment. If you ski where the snow is wet or where the mountains sometimes get winter rains, you'll want your ski clothing to be waterproof. If you ski where it's very cold, down or other high-loft insulation is desirable. If you snowboard, look for extra-tough fabric, especially on the knees, elbows and seat. Most ski and snowboard clothing is ruggedly made. Even midrange clothing has such "performance features" as storm cuffs, pit zips and a high or lined collar.

Remember, unless you are skiing Aspen or Sun Valley in high season or flitting off to top Alpine resorts where people do dress in very high style, you don't even need to think about this year's silhouette or next year's color. You just need garments that are the right size and offer protection and performance while you're skiing.

CHAPTER FOUR

FAMILY VALUES

Skiing is the ultimate family sport. Large ski resorts and small local areas alike compete fiercely for the family trade with a variety of programs and facilities: nurseries to care for infants and preskiing children, ski instruction for children, racing and freestyle programs to keep young skiers and snowboarders interested in the sport and even family-oriented après-ski to reduce the financial sting. When it comes to options that involve youngsters, "value" is often as important as a low sticker price. A day in a nursery or children's ski school may cost a significant amount at a pricey resort, but if it enables both parents to enjoy their own skiing, it's probably worth every cent.

NURSERIES AND DAY CARE CENTERS

As much as you love your wee one, you probably don't want to tend to your baby or toddler for the duration of your ski day, weekend or vacation. So that parents are free to ski, areas have entered the child care business. Ski country is full of safe, cheery nurseries, day care centers and playschools that rival or outdo many urban and suburban centers. Those few ski areas not offering supervision for young children can normally supply a list of recommended centers and sitters. State regulations are scrupulously followed in terms of minimum ages, ratio of caregivers to children, physical facilities and a slew of other requirements. When no ski area in a state accepts, say, infants, it is probably due to state prohibition.

Prices range wildly, and the country's most expensive nurseries are roughly twice as expensive as the most economical. When comparison shopping, take into consideration lift-ticket costs for adults and ski-age youngsters and kids-free policies (see pages 52-53) and day care for preskiers. Rates may be for hourly, half-day, full-day or multiday care. Parents generally need to supply diapers, formula and food for infants. Day care centers for toddlers and preschoolers often include snacks and lunches in their rates. At peak periods, reservations are recommended and often required.

Occasionally, child care is inexpensive or even free. Stratton, Vermont, provides reduced-rate day care (or Little Cub/Big Cub lessons) in conjunction with Ladies' Days on nonholiday Tuesdays and Gents' Days on Wednesdays. Smugglers' Notch leads the parade with free care for preskiers during selected family packages several times during the ski season or to guests of specific lodging properties. The resort's charming French restaurant, Le Cheval D'Or, picks up the tab for evening supervision at Alice's Wonderland Child Care Center for one child per family so that parents may dine in an adult atmosphere. The longest-running program is at Jay Peak, Vermont. Guests at the Hotel Jay or resort condominiums may tap into free care for children aged two to seven. Hours are a generous 9 A.M. to 9 P.M., so it's equally suitable for skiing or dinner. One of Crested Butte's largest condominium complexes, called Chateaux, offers free babysitting one evening a week. Ragged Mountain, New Hampshire, extends free lodging to children or half-price nursery care on midweek packages. When you ski Gore Mountain, New York, on Parents' Day (non-holiday Tuesdays), you get an adult lift ticket, a group ski lesson, child care for ages two to eight and a light snack for one low price. Colorado's Eldora Mountain Resort promotes a Mom's Monday package, comprising a series of five afternoons of lift, lesson and rentals for moms and Little MAC (Monday Afternoon Club) for children aged four to six.

CHILDREN'S SKI SCHOOLS AND CLUBS

Most ski areas offer lessons for children as young as three or four years old. As with nursery care, this can be an excellent investment. Not only does it free parents to ski, but it means that youngsters are introduced to skiing with their peers. Adults not emotionally attached to your child introduce him or her to the basic skills of sliding, turning and stopping. At the end of the day, you can check your child out of ski school and take a run or two. The "family zones" or "slow skiing trails" introduced on many mountains are the perfect places to start skiing as a family. When you ski together comfortably, you might consider that your youngster has "graduated" to skiing with you. Children's ski lessons can pack a financial wallop compared with the size of the skier and the amount of time he or she actually spends skiing, but Okemo softens the blow with a ten dollar Introduction to Skiing add-on for three- and four-year-olds enrolled in the nursery. Alpine Meadows, California, encourages youngsters to keep improving with a free lift ticket to children aged six to twelve taking a two-hour lesson. Bear Valley,

California, has a Frequent Skiing Bears deal with a fourth visit free after three paid days in the four- to eight-year-olds' program.

SKIwee, a franchised teaching program for children, includes standardized teaching methods and vocabulary of ski terms, plus a daily "report card" to help parents monitor their children's progress. This national program is currently available at eighty-six large and small ski areas across the country. Children who want to snowboard can enroll in MINIriders, which is organized along the same lines and is available at thirty-three ski areas. In all cases, instructors from each area's ski school follow the SKIwee or MINIrider curriculum. This provides the consistency that is beneficial to many children. It is a real plus if you normally ski near home, but take a family vacation at a destination resort once a year and don't want your children to lose ground between their home hill and the vacation resort. In addition to these pluses, SKIwee sponsors often provide value-added extras for skiing families, including product sampling and discounts.

Sunbelt families who ski figure that snowbelt families have it made. Snow-country school systems sponsor learn-to-ski programs in conjunction with physical education requirements or as an extracurricular elective. Middle schools and high schools might field racing and freestyle teams for serious skiers and snowboarders. Ski areas also offer series of weekend lift-and-lesson programs geared to local youngsters. Packages often include supervised bus transportation from the nearest city, lifts, lessons and perhaps lunch. The Eskimo Ski Club, founded in 1939, is the oldest such program in the country. Three generations of Denver youngsters have learned to ski at Winter Park, and other programs are found elsewhere. These may not always be bargains, but they generally provide excellent value in terms of rapid progress—and they give children something to do on winter Saturdays.

If you live in a town with a ski area, your children will probably have access to free or bargain skiing, either as part of their school physical-education class or as an extracurricular activity. Grand County, Colorado, has a four-day school week so that youngsters can ski each Monday at Winter Park, where they get a free all-day ski lesson. Mammoth Lakes students ski free and get free lessons at Mammoth Mountain. Even kids in as small a town as Wallace, Idaho, and the surrounding area have enjoyed free ski school at nearby Lookout Pass for half-a-century. Students in Stowe and Colorado's Summit County may take extended classes in fall and spring so that they can have winter days off to train and compete. Lake Placid school children receive subsidized instruction and coaching in Alpine and Nordic skiing—and luge and bobsled, too. Steamboat Springs schools have enjoyed a longtime relationship with the Howelsen Ski Area. Those within a fifty-mile radius of Burke Mountain, Vermont, get lifts and lessons for nominal cost.

BEST DEALS FOR FAMILIES

Preschoolers or thereabouts ski free at most areas, but other children are often eligible for freebies too. The usual requirement is that the free child's ticket accompanies the purchase of an adult lift ticket, which means you can't drop a carload of kids off at the mountain while you amuse yourself elsewhere. Sometimes free skiing is on a one-on-one basis, meaning one child free per paying adult. Other times, a parent may bring more than one child. A paid lift ticket generally is required for children from age five or six to twelve, but you'll need to check the fine print to see exactly for what age range children's rates are valid. Some ski areas charge a low rate for children "under twelve" while others extend it as far as "age thirteen and under," a fine point but nevertheless one that can make a big difference in your annual skiing budget for the year or two your child falls into that category.

Family tickets are another way to save. Whitetail, Pennsylvania, offers a special deal on a lift ticket for at least one adult and one youngster to age nineteen on Sundays and for night skiing. The Family Night version also nets each child a three dollar discount on food. Though it's part of the Mt. Snow/Killington/Sugarloaf family, Haystack, Vermont, doesn't get the traffic of its larger partners, so it floats Budget Saturday and Sunday with lift tickets for two adults and two children at a rate thrifty parents love. Mt. Rose, Nevada, is popular with local families for its Runs & Roses ticket. SilverCreek, Colorado, offers both day skiing on an economical Family Passport and a really inexpensive family season pass option. Black Mountain, New Hampshire, issues an economical Family Passport for two adults and two children, valid any day including holidays. Alyeska, Alaska, even more generously prices its version for two adults and two children to age seventeen.

In addition to Diamond Peak, Nevada's long-running family pack of two adults' and two children's day tickets for one economical price, this congenial family-oriented resort recognizes that these days, a "family" isn't necessarily based on a two-adult household. The Single Parent Package is therefore based on one adult and one child. On both, additional children in the family are eligible for a nominal add-on. The resort also offers a skip-a-generation day-skiing deal for one or two grandparents aged sixty or over and up to four grandchildren aged six to twelve. At nearby Alpine Meadows, California, Family Pak options can be based on one or two

BEST DEALS FOR CHILDREN

SKI AREA	THE DEAL (USUALLY WITH PURCHASE OF ADULT TICKET)
Arizona Snowbowl, AZ	Free skiing for age 7 and under
Big Sky, MT	Free skiing for age 10 and under (2 per adult)
Boyne Highlands, Boyne Mountain, MI	Free skiing for age 8 and under
Bretton Woods, NH	Children 6 to 15 pay their age (Monday through Friday)
Brighton, UT	Free skiing for age 10 and under (2 per adult)
Camelback, PA	Children 46 inches tall and under ski free
Cascade Mountain, WI	Children 10 and under ski free on novice lifts
Crested Butte, CO	12 and under pay their age
Dodge Ridge, CA	Free skiing for age 8 and under
Homewood, CA	Free skiing for age 8 and under
Hunter Mountain, NY	Free skiing for age 12 and under (midweek, nonholiday)
King Ridge, NH	Free skiing on Fridays for age 12 and under
Kirkwood, CA	Very low-cost ticket for ages 6 to 12
Mountain High, CA	Free skiing for age 9 and under
Mt. Waterman, CA	Free skiing for age 11 and under
Nub's Nob, MI	Free skiing for age 8 and under
Porcupine Mountains, MI	Free skiing for age 12 and under
Purgatory Resort, CO	Unrestricted free skiing for age 12 and under
Rib Mountain, WI	Second child under 13 free with paying adult (midweek, nonholiday)
Sandia Peak, NM	Free skiing for child under 46 inches in height
Ski Brule and Ski Homestead, MI	Free skiing for age 9 and under

Ski Windham, NY	Free skiing for age 12 and younger when accompanying an adult, nonholiday mid-weeks
Skyline Ski Area, MI	Free skiing on beginner hill for age 8 and under
Snowbird, UT	Free skiing for age 12 and under (up to two children per adult) using chairlifts; additional fee to ride tram
Squaw Valley USA, CA	Ultra low-cost ticket for age 12 and under

adults and one or two children. Any grandparent who enrolls one child in the Bolton Valley, Vermont, children's ski school receives his or her own ticket for a junior rate; two children nets a free ticket. Ski Windham, New York, offers single-parent packages several weeks during the ski season. Killington, Vermont, is one of a handful of areas promoting a family ski lesson for up to five people of various ages. After a five-day program at Angel Fire, New Mexico's, children's program, the last day is free.

TEEN TACTICS

As your child enters the teen years, the financial sledding becomes rough. Not only will your child outgrow clothing and footwear with alarming speed *and* eat everything in the kitchen except the refrigerator, but you're suddenly hit with an adult tab for everything from movie tickets to bus fares. While most ski areas extend children's rates to age twelve or thirteen, some ease the financial crush for parents of teens with teen or student tickets, which may be more than children's rates but are still less than adults'. Most are small areas, but a surprising number of sizable mountains also have a teen price category for day tickets. Even Steamboat, which brought the concept of free skiing for children to the forefront, now has a teen ticket category for vacationing families. A few ski areas simply raise the top age of a child's ticket; this policy is more common in Canada than in the United States. In fact, Canada is a hotbed of cool deals for teens. Children's rates commonly extended to age fourteen, and occasionally even to seventeen or eighteen, are not all that unusual, especially in eastern Canada. Top western resorts often have teen rates from age thirteen to seventeen or eighteen. Here is a sampling of some teen deals available in recent seasons at resorts of various sizes.

UNITED STATES

SKI AREA	TEEN/STUDENT RATES FOR . . .
Afton Alps, MN	13 to 17
Antelope Butte, WY	Child rate to age 15
Ascutney Mountain Resort, VT	Child rate to age 16
The Big Mountain, MT	13 to 18
Black Mountain, NH	Child rate to age 15
Boyne Highlands, MI	13 to 19
Bretton Woods, NH	Ages 6 to 15 pay their age (Monday through Friday)
Bridger Bowl, MT	13 to 18
Bromley Mountain, VT	Child rate to age 14
Brundage, ID	13 to 18
Buck Hill, MN	12 to 18
Burke Mountain, VT	Child rate to age 16
Christie Mountain, WI	12 to 18
Copper Mountain, CO	Child rate to age 14; additional low-cost lift tickets for 3 days or more
Crystal Mountain, WA	12 to 17
Diamond Peak, NV	13 to 17 on Family Special rates
Grand Targhee, WY	Child rate to age 14
Haystack, VT	Age 13 through college with valid ID
Heavenly Ski Resort, CA/NV	13 to 15
Highmount Ski Center, NY	10 to 15
Hunter Mountain, NY	13 to 18 and college students with valid ID
Indianhead, MI	13 to 17
June Mountain, CA	13 to 18
Kirkwood, CA	13 to 24
Lookout Pass, ID	Child rate to age 18
Mammoth Mountain, CA	13 to 18
Mission Ridge, WA	Child rate to age 15; also 16 to 20 rate (weekend savings)
Mohawk Mountain, CT	Child rate to age 15
Mt. Ashaway, WI	Child rate through high school
Mt. Bachelor, OR	13 to 17

Mt. Baker, WA	Child rate to age 16
Mt. La Crosse, WI	11 to 17
Mt. Waterman, CA	12 to 15
Northstar-at-Tahoe, CA	13 to 20 on Club Vertical membership
Okemo, VT	13 to 18
Pico Ski Resort, VT	Child rate to age 14
Schweitzer Mountain Resort, ID	Child rate to age 17
Shanty Creek, MI	13 to 17
Silver Mountain, ID	13 to 17
Smugglers' Notch, VT	Child rate to age 17 on multiday packages
Snowhill at Eastman, NH	Child rate to age 17
Snow Summit, CA	2 tiers, 13 to 18 and 19 to 22 (midweek only)
Spirit Mountain, MN	Child rate to age 15
Steamboat, CO	13 to 15 for lift-ticket savings when family stays 5 nights or longer in participating property
Sugarloaf USA, ME	13 to 18
Terry Peak, SD	Child rate to age 17
Treetops Sylvan Resort, MI	Child rate to age 17
Welch Village, MN	Child rate to age 17
Wild Mountain, MN	Child rate to age 17

CANADA

SKI AREA	TEEN/STUDENT RATES FOR . . .
Apex Resort, BC	13 to 18
Big White Resort, BC	13 to 17
Blackcomb, BC	13 to 17
Fairmont Hot Springs, BC	Child rate to age 14
Fernie Snow Valley, BC	13 to 17
Grande Coulee, QU	Child rate to age 19
Grouse Mountain, BC	13 to 18
Harper Mountain, BC	Child rate to age 14
Hemlock Valley Resorts, BC	13 to 17
Le Mont Grands Fonds, QU	13 to 23 (student)
Le Relais, QU	13 to 23 (student)

Manning Ski Resort, BC	13 to 17
Marmot-Baldy, BC	Child rate to age 14, then 15 to 18 student rate
Marmot Basin, AB	13 to 17
Mont. Fortin, QU	Child/student rate to age 23
Montjoye, QU	Child rate to age 15, then 16 to 21 student rate
Mont Orford, QU	Student rate to age 23
Mont Original, QU	Child rate to age 17
Mont Ste.-Anne, QU	14 to 20
Mont Tribasse, QU	Child rate to age 17
Mont Video, QU	13 to 23
Mt. Washington Ski Resort, BC	13 to 18
Mystic Ridge and Norquay, AB	13 to 17
Nakiska, AB	13 to 17
Red Mountain, BC	13 to 18
Silver Star Mountain, BC	13 to 17
Ski Smithers, BC	13 to 18
Ski Stoneham, QU	Child rate to age 15, then student rate 16 to 22
Sun Peaks, BC	13 to 18
Sunshine Village, AB	13 to 17
Vallée du Parc, QU	Child rate to age 20
Westcastle Park, AB	13 to 17
Whistler Mountain, BC	13 to 17
Whitewater, BC	13 to 18

BEATING THE HIGH COST OF SERIOUS SKIING

If your child becomes serious about ski racing, competitive snowboarding or freestyle competition, you can kiss the new car or perhaps even the college fund good-bye—unless he or she gets so good that the U.S. Ski Team beckons. More likely, you'll have a teenager who loves to ski or snowboard but does not enjoy that stratospheric skill level. Season passes and teen tickets help cut the costs, but there are other ways, too. Local ski areas often have part-time jobs open to teens, but even if your child is younger, there are possibilities to turn that love of skiing into lift-ticket savings.

If your child is twelve to fifteen years old and is a strong intermediate skier or better, have him or her investigate Junior Ski Patrol or Junior Instructor positions at your local ski area. Patrollers must complete a winter emergency care course offered by the National Ski Patrol to learn first aid, rescue, chair evacuation and toboggan handling. Instructors take clinics in teaching beginners and small children and often help with entry-level classes. In exchange for about forty hours a month helping adult patrollers and instructors, they get free skiing, uniforms and the cachet that comes with working at a ski area.

Junior instructors observe classes and assist instructors, especially with beginner classes. Both skiing and snowboarding openings may be available. Youngsters may be asked to escort new skiers to the beginner area, demonstrate the skills that are being taught and assist new skiers in getting on and off the lift. They also often help with children's classes, setting up and dismantling terrain gardens, helping little ones with equipment, playing skis-on games with small skiers and serving as a buddy on the slope and on the lift. Training, lift tickets and uniforms are the most common benefits. Many ski areas, especially smaller ones, welcome fourteen and fifteen year olds in such programs. Monarch, Colorado, was so anxious to introduce teenagers to ski instruction that the ski school set up a cooperative program with the local 4-H Club. It's appropriately called the Farm Team.

BUDGET FAMILY VACATIONING

Most ski areas offer free skiing for children to about age six, and some destination resorts do even better, offering both free skiing and free lodging for children twelve and under during nonholiday periods. Of all the money-saving strategies you can employ (see "Stretching Your Ski-Vacation Dollar," page 60), finding free lodging and free skiing for youngsters is one of the most effective cost-cutting measures. Steamboat, Colorado's, landmark Kids Ski Free has offered free lodging when children share accommodations with their parents, free lift tickets and even free rentals (both on a one-on-one basis with parents) for children twelve and under since 1982. There are caveats, including a holiday blackout period and a minimum number of overnights at a participating lodging property. Nevertheless, more than ten thousand children each winter now ski, sleep and sometimes rent equipment free at Steamboat.

A host of imitators have followed with variations on the Kids Ski Free theme. Some have virtually copied the program, and some have expanded it. Among those values recently available for families, a standout is Purgatory, Colorado's, unconditional free skiing for children aged twelve and under, as well as free lodging in some properties. Children twelve and under ski free with an adult paying full price for a lift ticket on nonholiday weekdays at Ski Windham, New York. Other programs for children twelve and under (unless noted otherwise) include free lodging for youngsters in their parents' room or unit at Snowbird, Utah, and free skiing when at least one parent purchases a lift ticket. At resorts as disparate as Belleayre, New York, and Indianhead, Michigan, children ski and stay free when the family overnights in a participating lodge. Red River, New Mexico, pegs the ratio at one child free per parent when the family stays in a participating lodge for three nights or longer. When coupled with the resort's Wednesday Free program and a Sunday or Monday check-in, two adults can vacation for four days for the price of three, and two children can coast along gratis. Sixteen New Hampshire areas participate in the Family Ski Pass program, which provides one free child's ticket with the purchase of an economical five-day adult pass during nonholiday midweeks. When you combine it with something like Attitash's kids-stay-free policy and a complimentary sleighride on five-night or longer packages, it makes a really nice family vacation. Similarly, when an adult uses a Ski Tahoe North interchangeable lift ticket at Diamond Peak, Nevada, the area provides a free child's ticket. Copper Mountain, Colorado, and Stratton, Vermont, offer free lodging and very inexpensive children's lift tickets to age fouteen on family stays of three days or longer. Copper and Grand Targhee, Wyoming, up the kids-free age limit on lodging and skiing to fourteen when parents buy a five-night Family Package. Two places in Idaho do even better, ratcheting the upper limit into the teens. At Sun Valley, youngsters to age fifteen get free lodging and skiing when the family stays at the Sun Valley Lodge, Sun Valley Inn or Lodge Condominiums. There's free skiing at Silver Mountain for children and teens to age seventeen and free lodging at Idaho's posh Coeur d'Alene Resort on family packages of two nights or longer. At Holiday Valley, New York, the top age for free lodging and skiing is also seventeen on midweek ski packages.

Some resorts go even further to court families. Smugglers' Notch, Vermont, has established a niche as a top family resort. Throughout the season, its entire Club Smugglers' is an inclusive package featuring a gamut of skiing and evening activities. Smugglers' also offers free child care for ages six weeks to two years on various packages for a time in December before Christmas and again in January, as well as free Ski Camps for three- to twelve-year-olds. FamilyFest, later in the season, carries such additional benefits as free children's rentals, half-price dinners at one of the resort's restaurants and a supervised children's dinner one evening so that parents can enjoy dinner on their own. To top it off, families booking six nights on the Club Smugglers' packages get a seventh night free. ExploreMore vacations at Waterville Valley, New Hampshire, include five nights' lodging, five days' skiing, an innkeeper's welcome party, a family ice skating party, animal presentations, family games night, kids' night out and a torchlight parade for one modest rate. They are available almost weekly from late January through late March. Other resorts create family vacation packages for selected weeks during the season. When all the components are considered, they are excellent values. Among the best are Teddy Bear Ski Weeks at Mt. Snow/Haystack, Vermont; SilverBear Ski Weeks at SilverCreek, Colorado; Winter Magic Weeks at Killington, Vermont; Family Weeks at Indianhead, Michigan; and M&M Mars Children's Festivals and Family Fling Weeks at Sugarloaf, Maine. Butternut Basin, Massachusetts, a smaller area, offers weekend equivalents called Kids Festivals and Family Fun Weekends. When a family books into the Lodge at Mt. Snow for a five-day package, youngsters not only stay and ski free, but eat free, too.

SEEK OUT FAMILY DEALS

Soft-drink bottlers, candy companies and fast-food chains sometimes float attractive family promotional deals. But few promotions spawn as good a deal as Family Ski Nights at Bristol Mountain, New York. With the presentation of a Wegman's Shoppers Club Card, skiers get reduced-rate family lift tickets on Saturday nights, half-price ski and snowboard rentals, free beginner lessons and even low-cost nursery care. The offer is valid for two parents and at least one child or one parent and at least two children. Many other promotional tie-ins, while not limited to families, are clearly directed at them (see "Ticket Tactics," page 10).

A FINAL WORD ON SKI EQUIPMENT AND CLOTHING

Children don't need the fanciest, most expensive ski gear on the market. But they need equipment that is current enough to be skiable and safe, and they do need clothing and such accessories as mittens and hats to keep them warm and dry. Buying new makes the most sense if you have two or more children to outfit. The younger ones are probably so accustomed to hand-me-downs that this won't be a problem for them. See "Gearing Up" (page 36) for ways to save money when you outfit your child.

CHAPTER FIVE

STRETCHING YOUR SKI-VACATION DOLLAR

Minding their wallets every day they ski is, for many people, but a warm-up for the annual winter vacation. Thrifty skiers view a trip as a one-week opportunity to save money. You can start by incorporating tactics you've found in other chapters of this book, including discount cards, low-season and midweek skiing (see "Ticket Tactics," page 10), kids-free offers (see "Family Values," page 48) and factoring both location and price into selecting your destination (see "Hidden Treasures," page 112).

Think of a ski vacation as a full-course meal. If you order your appetizer, soup, salad, entrée and dessert from the à la carte menu, you'll pay more than you would for a complete dinner. Likewise, if you book your airline ticket, rental car or shuttle van, accommodations, lift tickets, rental equipment and ski lessons separately, you'll pay much more than you would for a package. "Package" is a travel industry term that means several components of a holiday are included in one price. Packages can be as basic as lodging-and-lifts combinations for drive-to destinations or comprehensive arrangements on an array of add-ons. No matter how you book them, they are the most efficient ways to save, but seasoned traveling skiers have other tricks up their sleeves, too.

HOW TO PLAN A SKI VACATION

To travel or not to travel, that is the skier's question. Is it better to ski close to home and ski as many days as possible or to seek more distant snows? For peripatetic types, there's no question that skiing nearby is but a prelude for pleasures found elsewhere. Travel planning is like a big matrix. You take your budget, list the elements and their options and figure out where you want to save and where you can spend.

As soon as you decide where you're going, you have to figure how to get there. The easiest and least expensive option is by car—especially for a family or group. The benefits slack off if you're a party of one or two or if you're traveling so far that driving simply isn't practical. In either case, you need to take to the air. Bargain airfares, often with a limited booking-and-paying window, have lured skiers into the skies in the recent past. Industry experts warn flyers not to expect such too-good-to-be-true deals in the near future, but you never know. Since ski season is off-season in most of the tourist industry, fares reduced by a quarter to a third could come along. If fares do plunge, grab them fast—and, if you are not already a member, be sure to enroll yourself and every member of your family in the airline's frequent flyer plan. It's free, miles do accumulate toward future tickets and other travel and special offers sometimes are mailed to members.

The option of train travel is a realistic one for skiers. Though Congress has cut them, Amtrak's routes still access the ski country of Vermont-New Hampshire, upstate New York, the upper Midwest, two routes each across the Great Plains and Rockies and the Sierra Nevada, Cascades and other Pacific states destinations. If your destination is at or near a major resort, an airport (or train station) shuttle is likely, but if not, a rental car is necessary. Like airline tickets, rates are not expected to drop in the near future. You can try to shop around for good deals (tie-ins with frequent flyer plans, discounts for belonging to AAA, advance-purchase rates and so forth), but more important than a bargain is to book a four-wheel or all-wheel drive car—or at least a front-wheel drive model with snow tires.

Where to stay? Most skiers today prefer modern accommodations, places with ample hot water, a decent kitchen, cable television, ice machines and various other home comforts. You might also find that a full-service hotel or a budget motel suits your needs. But there are other options. For congeniality and charm, in short, the essence of a winter vacation, nothing beats a country lodge. You'll find casual comfort, good food, congenial company and skiing outside the door. If that kind of atmosphere appeals to you, you might also consider a dude ranch. Winter is off-season, so rates are low, and all-inclusive packages are likely to include skiing and other winter sports. Accommodations with housekeeping facilities (that is, kitchen and perhaps laundry facilities) can save money and be perfect for a family or group.

To compare costs, use toll-free numbers to get price quotes for air or rail tickets, rental car or other ground transportation and accommodations and construct a table (of course, filling in dollar figures) of variables that would look something like this:

TRANSPORTATION	ACCOMMODATIONS	MEALS
Car (including gas and tolls)	Condominium	Included in lodging cost
Air or rail (including ground transportation)	Hotel or motel	Dining out
	Lodge or B&B	Preparing your own
	Other	

SKIING	MISCELLANEOUS
Lift tickets	Entertainment
Rentals	Child care
Ski lessons	Nonski activities

Fill in each line with the rate quotes you've gotten and the estimates for such optionals and imponderables as meals and entertainment. Sharpen your pencil or reload your calculator. Add them up in various combinations, remembering to multiply the appropriate categories by the number of people in your group. Build in a fudge factor of 10 or 15 percent either way. You'll have a reasonably good idea of what your total ski-vacation costs will be, and it may surprise you how little difference there is in the total cost of various options.

TRAVEL INSURANCE

To snare the best possible airfares, you'll probably book airline tickets that are impossible or expensive to change, and if you read the fine print in the tour operators' program or your lodging contract, you may find a no-refund policy. Ski vacationing is full of what-if's that can be expensive. What if your child comes down with strep throat? What if your baggage is lost, seriously delayed or wrecked? What if the airline goes on strike or even folds, the tour operator goes under or you total the rental car?

You can buy travel insurance to cover such contingencies, but in the interest of economy, it makes sense to weigh the probable risks you'll encounter and figure out what kind of protection you'll need. Factor in the insurance that you already have and also your willingness to assume some financial risk for other problems that might arise. Your health and homeowner's policies may already cover many potential mishaps, including accidents, illnesses or property loss, so read those policies or call your insurance agent before you buy additional coverage.

If you charge your trip on a major credit card, especially the gold or platinum variety, many of the mishaps or failures may be covered. For example, the credit card will probably also pick up the hefty deductible for a rental car accident until your auto insurance kicks in. This will enable you to decline the costly collision damage coverage that car rental firms sell at a high per-day cost. Your homeowner's insurance will help if your baggage disappears, because airlines are liable for a maximum of fifteen hundred dollars per loss for checked baggage, and that normally won't cover costly ski equipment and clothing.

If you want further protection, you may buy special travel insurance for such other emergencies as trip cancellation or interruptions, medical evacuation flights, medical or dental emergencies, replacement of lost travel documents and travel or baggage delays beyond what the airline covers.

When an insurance company sets its premiums according to the price of the trip, expect to pay about $110 for a $2,000 vacation. When a company charges by the time period, you'll pay about $110 comprehensive coverage on a nine- to fifteen-day trip. Benefits typically include $100 for delayed baggage, $500 for travel delays, $10,000 for medical expenses and $20,000 for emergency medical assistance. Some plans also cover hospitalization, collision damage (which is useful for urbanites who may not have their own car but rent one on vacation) and accidental death or dismemberment. Insurance companies do offer different levels of coverage, and some also have family plans that cut the per-person cost.

You can purchase a policy as an add-on to your vacation from your travel agent or tour operator or directly from an insurance company. These 800 numbers may be designated to sign up new customers, serve as emergency hotlines and provide claims and other services, so you may be on hold for a while: Access America (800-499-9200), Carefree Travel Insurance (800-645-2424), Health Care Abroad (800-237-6615), International SOS Assistance (800-523-8930), Travel Assistance International (800-821-2828), Travel Guard (800-782-5151), Travel Insured International (800-243-3174), TravMed (800-732-5309) and Trip Mate Insurance (800-888-7292).

SAVINGS START WITH GOOD RESEARCH

Read guidebooks, ski publications and the special ski sections that appear in many newspapers in the fall. Spend a few hours at a consumer ski show (see "Ticket Tactics," page 10), collect literature and pump the salespeople for information about their resort. Use the toll-free numbers maintained by ski resorts' central reservations operations, tour operators, airlines and any other travel providers you might be using to gather information. If you want a comprehensive directory of these 800 numbers, call (800) 426-8686 and order the *AT&T 800 Travel Directory*. Find a travel agent who skis—or at least is knowledgeable about ski resorts. The more you know to begin with, the better you'll be able to discern excellent values when you come across them.

SKI THE INTERNET

Travel providers marketing through specific on-line services—the Internet or the World Wide Web—are beginning to proliferate in sports travel as well as other areas. Once you are wired into the information superhighway, you can do some basic research and even find good vacation deals. In spite of the hype, the so-called superhighway is still more of a network of local streets, dead ends and country roads. There's no atlas, and it's easy to get lost and frustrated.

Still, if you have a computer and a modem, you can access a world of skiing and travel information. The census of cyber-sources is increasing with lightning speed. More competition and a growing market have caused rates to drop. Many ski resorts, ski areas, state tourism associations and other travel providers have set up their own home pages on the Internet or the World Wide Web and more will continue to do so. The National Ski Areas Association has set up a web site (http://www.travelbase.com/ skiareas) in an effort to provide a directory of and hyperlink to other ski and snowboard web sites, and The Skiing Company, which publishes *Skiing* and *Ski*, has established SkiNet. This web site incorporates travel planning, equipment reviews and news from both magazines' pages, as well as other services at http://www.skinet.com/. In addition, special-interest "forums" enable you to trade direct information with other skiers and travelers. You might even be able to rent a bargain condominium through an on-line contact.

If you subscribe to an on-line service, you can use your computer to obtain information that many resorts now post, and you can also trade tips on the travel or special-interest forums with other skiers. These services still provide the easiest routes to ski and travel information. Popular computer magazines are stuffed with free floppy disks that you can use to test various systems. Otherwise, call the phone numbers below for more information or to join. When you join and provide your credit card number for billing purposes, you will be given a local number or an 800 number to link into to communicate with the system. The leading services are America OnLine (800-827-6364), CompuServe (800-848-8199), Delphi (800-695-4005), GEnie (800-638-9636) and Microsoft Network (supplied with Windows95). Of these, AOL currently has the most comprehensive travel and ski forums. Other computer information sources are available too. TravelBank Systems (303-745-8586; modem 303-671-7669) started out giving on-line ski reports for Colorado. It now includes pricing information and even discount coupons that you can print out for lodging, dining and other services in ski country.

TOUR OPERATORS AND CENTRAL RESERVATIONS SERVICES

If you don't belong to a ski club, you can still take advantage of group purchasing power by booking a vacation package either directly from the provider or through your travel agent. At the very least, a ski-vacation package will include accommodations and lift tickets. Unless you are driving, you will need such "add-ons" as air and ground transportation. The biggest savings from a package come in these areas. Bulk purchasers such as tour operators and travel agencies negotiate significantly cheaper airfares than consumers can get by simply calling the airline directly. Sometimes, they also get volume reductions on lift tickets, lodging, rentals and other services.

Ground transportation might be a shuttle from the airport to the resort or a rental car. Unless it is included in your package, you need to weigh your options. You have to divide your rental car (plus gas, tolls and possibly insurance) by the number of people in your party and multiply the van or bus fare by that number. If you are going to a very small resort or a very large one with a free bus system, you probably won't need a car at all while you are there. If, on the other hand, you are saving money by staying in a remote location, you'll need a car to get around. Other add-ons, including ski instruction and child care, may not necessarily be less expensive simply because they are quasi-packaged, but there is a degree of efficiency in arranging everything with one call.

If you know where you want to vacation, a toll-free call to the resort's 800 central reservations number is easy (see "Appendix," page 148). Many now operate as "full-service travel agencies" with the ability to book your airline ticket, rental car and other off-site services. At all major and some smaller resorts, you can reserve rental equipment, ski lessons, child care and perhaps even some evening activities. The advantage of going directly to resorts is that they have the inside track to their own facilities. The disadvantage is that if they cannot book the dates and accommodations you want, they obviously are knowledgeable only about that one place, and you'll have to make another call to your second-choice destination.

If you are undecided about your destination or plan to travel at peak periods when availability may be limited, tour operators specializing in ski travel have a wider range of choices to a number of resorts. They may specialize in a particular region or work with areas all over the country. If you go through an airline-linked tour operator, such as Delta Dream Vacations or Continental Grand Destinations, packages are obviously only available to resorts that can be reached from its gateways. You may be offered additional benefits. For instance, ski rental shops may offer discounts to clients of specific tour operators.

Operators might also add incentives of their own to entice you to book the packages through them. For example, Any Mountain Tours (800-296-2000) traditionally offers lodging discounts of up to 30 percent for clients who finalize their ski vacations between August 15 and September 30. Daman-Nelson (800-343-2626) offers added value to families booking its popular Sun Valley packages with a free half-day lesson for children twelve and under and a variety of free or low-cost off-slope activities. Adventure Travel Specialists (800-SKI-TRIP) guarantees the lowest-priced package at the time of booking or they will refund double the difference. The Colorado Vacation Club (800-866-0717), a tour operator marketing through a membership format, sends new clients a seventy-five dollar vacation voucher and also knocks one hundred dollars off the first package they book.

When you have selected your package, read the fine print on the tour brochure before you confirm your booking. Be sure you understand payment deadlines and cancellation penalties. Unless it is included in your package, consider trip-cancellation insurance. While most tour operators are scrupulously reliable, paying by credit card gives you another layer of financial protection if the company goes out of business, the airline is grounded or some other serious problem develops.

If you worry about falling into the hands of a fly-by-night tour operator, you might want to start with a company that belongs to a specialty trade association. Only companies in business for at least five years and generating at least 10,000 overnights annually are allowed to join SkiTops, which is short for Ski Tour Operators Association. You can send for a list by writing to SkiTops, P.O. Box 3158, Englewood, CO 80158-3158. Other leading ski-tour operators belong to the National Ski Tour Operators Association, which also can supply members' names. Contact NASTOA, 1012 South Cleveland Street, Arlington, VA 22204; (703) 979-4300.

THE NITTY-GRITTY

Eventually you have to stop researching and start booking your ski trip. The main choices you'll have to make are transportation, destination, time and duration of your trip. If you decide on a ski-club trip or another program with limited departures, some of these choices are made for you. Otherwise, you need to plow ahead, and, as with skiing in general, you'll have to make trade-offs to save money.

THE TRANSPORTATION TANGLE

If you live within striking distance of your vacation destination, you might opt for driving your own car. Especially for a family holiday, this is a far more economical option than the price of an airline ticket times the number of people in your family. You'll have to budget for fuel, meals on the road, possibly tolls and perhaps even an overnight, with contingencies for bad weather and poor road conditions. You also need to consider the wear and tear of driving. Will you be relaxed when you get home, or will you be weary from the long return trip? If time is money or you simply have too little vacation time or live too far from your destination to consider driving, you'll have to bite the monetary bullet and buy an airline ticket.

FLY THE FRUGAL SKIES   Passengers seated in the back of the plane arrive at the same time as those in the front. Except for the extras in first class, you get the same food, beverages, baggage handling and attention of the flight attendants regardless of how much or how little you've paid for your ticket. Therefore, it makes no sense to spend any more on airline travel than you have to. If there's a fare war, take advantage of it. If you find special introductory fares, grab them. Whether you choose a mainline airline, such as American, Continental, Delta, Northwest or United, or a low-fare start-up like the ones on page 68, sign on for the frequent flyer program and begin to accrue miles. You'll be able to use them for future travel.

Colorado, the country's number-one ski state, has been hit with an air revolution since 1993. Denver was once the automatic port of entry for skiers into the state, and in recent years, direct flights from key coastal and Midwestern cities to Aspen, Durango (for Purgatory), Eagle (for Vail and Beaver Creek), Gunnison (for Crested Butte), Hayden (for Steamboat) and Telluride (or Montrose, where flights were frequently diverted in bad weather) have offered skiers convenient alternative air options. Several factors in the early 1990s changed the nature of air travel to Colorado. The well-publicized and expensive opening of Denver International Airport spurred an increase in landing fees and therefore higher airfares. Continental Airline's concurrent retreat from the Denver market granted United Airlines a virtual monopoly of Denver, which they used to raise fares still more. Finally, the reduction of service to several mountain airports cut available seats to the mountains.

If you can snag a seat on a low-fare carrier, that's more money in your pocket. Southwest Airlines, which serves such ski gateways as Salt Lake City, Colorado Springs, Reno and Albuquerque, packages well-priced ski trips under the name Fun Pack Vacations (800-423-5683) in conjunction with its trend-setting fare structure. Taking a leaf from Southwest's book, Western Pacific Airlines (800-930-3030), also offers low fares and flies to Colorado Springs. Reno Airlines has excellent service from various Western cities to its namesake hub, gateway to the Lake Tahoe ski resorts. Vanguard Airlines' route system includes both Denver and Salt Lake City. Frontier Airlines hubs in Denver, with service to the Midwest, Plains States and other states in the Rocky Mountain region. Some newer carriers like Southwest and Pacific Western have initially eschewed DIA for Colorado Springs, which is a viable and often economical choice, especially if you are heading to Summit County, Monarch or Crested Butte, and most especially if you are planning to rent a car.

With the problems at DIA, Salt Lake City and Reno gleefully promoted their all-weather airports, good airfares and proximity to great skiing. But the airline industry is fickle, and what was true yesterday might change today and be history by tomorrow. Whatever is going on in air travel, a seat that hasn't been taken is the spoiled goods of travel, and airlines always seek to pack planes. Therefore, airlines drop fares to make travel more attractive, and "consolidators" sell discounted tickets from excess seat inventory to international and domestic destinations. To get the best fares, no matter where you're going, you may need to be flexible in your travel plans. You can find consolidators' small-print ads in the Sunday travel sections of major newspapers. They are also increasingly using the Internet and the Web to market available flights.

Skiers heading for a limited number of ski destinations have the Amtrak option too. While train travel is rarely inexpensive, is time-consuming and, because of the limited passenger service in this country, is inflexible, it is an add-on adventure that some skiers find priceless. You can take Amtrak to Salt Lake City with easy access to many Utah ski areas. Some smaller stations are located at or near ski resorts, too. For instance, you can take the train to Granby, Colorado, for Winter Park and SilverCreek; to Glenwood Springs, Colorado, for Ski Sunlight and Aspen/Snowmass; to Whitefish for The Big Mountain, Montana; and to Sandpoint, Idaho, for Schweitzer Mountain Resort. Amtrak keeps tinkering with its schedules in the Northeast, but ski resorts near Vermont's White River Junction and Essex Junction have traditionally tapped into the rail travelers' market. In addition, weekend ski trains operate between Denver and Winter Park and between Portland, Maine, and Sunday River, and skiers can use them for vacations too. In Canada, Banff is a major rail stop as well as a major ski destination.

LODGING LOCATION COUNTS

When you're selecting a condo or lodge, consider location as much as style and level of luxury. If you are close to the lifts, you'll probably get on the hill earlier, and you might even be able to ski "home" for lunch instead of buying one on the mountain. Unless you are within walking distance of the slopes, you'll need wheels to get there. If you fly to your ski vacation destination, you should consider whether you need a rental car. If you do, all other things being equal, look for agencies with such value-added bonuses as a free ski rack, unlimited mileage or even a free lift ticket to a choice of areas. If the resort has a free shuttle-bus service, as most resorts now do, you won't need a car at all, and an airport shuttle might be cheaper than having your rental sitting around day after day while you ski. On some packages, you have ground transportation options, including rental car and van or bus shuttle. If you are staying in an outlying town to save money and do drive to the ski area, you will need wheels, but if you're dealing with an automobile, remember to factor in the parking fee charged at many destination resorts for the most convenient lots or garages.

SLEEP IN THE CITY . . .   A handful of cities near big-time ski areas often offer excellent air service, exceptional lodging deals and, in some cases, fabulously priced ski packages. While the urban experience does not replicate that of a ski resort, it does offer great value, outstanding services and an abundance of things to do. In addition to the economy of such vacation strategy, you can really feel like a local skier, leaving "home" in the morning for a daytrip to a nearby mountain resort and returning after the lifts close. In the city, you will find a great range of restaurants and après-ski activities from the traditional dining/dancing/partying to such cosmopolitan diversions as theater, concerts or major-league sports. With their abundance of hotels and motels for business travelers and convention-goers, big cities also may offer the only good lodging buys and ample availability during peak holiday seasons.

You can make the city your vacation spot of choice, or you might be able to turn a business trip into a mini-vacation with some planning and a day or two between meetings when you can schedule mental-health time on skis. Your company may even appreciate your "volunteering" to stay over a Saturday night to get a lower airfare. Often, you won't even need a car to escape to the slopes, though you might have to do some creative air routing. Denver and Salt Lake City offer easy day-hopping and serve as midcontinent airline hubs. (Areas below that are marked with an asterisk offer night skiing, too.)

A couple of U.S. cities are real standouts for skiers. Salt Lake City, designated host for the 2002 Winter Olympics, has the most organized ski-and-stay program, the best access to world-class skiing and a wide selection of accommodations in various price ranges. Some properties offer traditional packages, while at others, discount lift tickets are sold at the front desk. With seven ski areas an hour or less away, Salt Lake City, Delta's western hub, is also very well set up for day-hopping business travelers. The public UTA Ski Bus (801-BUS-INFO) runs frequent, low-cost service from downtown hotels to Alta and Snowbird in Little Cottonwood Canyon and Brighton and Solitude in Big Cottonwood Canyon. Lewis Bros. Stages (800-826-5844) is a private company with scheduled buses from city hotels to the Park City ski areas (Park City*, Deer Valley and Wolf Mountain) and those in Big Cottonwood Canyon. Several of the city's larger hotels have enough business ambiance to ease your conscience but provide other services for skiing convenience. In addition to equipment, you can rent ski clothing in town from Ski-N-See (800-722-3685), Utah Ski Rental (801-355-9088) and Canyon Sports (801-539-8410). The Salt Lake City Convention & Visitors Bureau (801-521-2822) issues a comprehensive visitor's guide that includes discount coupons for ski rentals, meals and other services.

Denver, a major United hub, also has an organized escape to the mountains that is more suited for a one-day escape than as a vacation hub. The Denver Ski Lift (800-283-2754) packages such components as van (or rental-car) transportation and a lift ticket at areas two hours or less from the city (Arapahoe Basin, Beaver Creek, Breckenridge, Copper, Eldora*, Keystone*, Loveland, SilverCreek, Vail and Winter Park) and can also arrange rental equipment (and even clothing). Because resort van services are prohibited from serving downtown hotels, you would otherwise need to return to the airport if you selected any other option. Loveland additionally offers a fantastic lift ticket/rental package that includes not just ski equipment but clothing and accessories too. It is aimed specifically at the business traveler with a day to ski.

Reno may not have a midcontinent location or be a big-time business destination, but it is the gateway to the fifteen Alpine and thirteen Nordic ski areas near Lake Tahoe and has positioned itself as a convenient and economical base for skiing on the North Shore. The Reno-Sparks Convention & Visitors Bureau (800-367-7366) issues a brochure listing more than a dozen properties from simple motels to elaborate casino-hotels that package lodging, lift-ticket vouchers and sometimes extras like dinner or a show. Some also offer complimentary airport shuttles. For those who prefer not to drive, Gray Line Tours (800-822-6009) packages accommodations, skiing at Squaw Valley and daily round-trip motor coach transportation to the mountain.

Major Pacific Northwest cities where you may find yourself on a business trip boast excellent skiing nearby. Mt. Hood Meadows, Mt. Hood Ski Bowl* and Timberline are sixty miles or less from Portland. Ticketmaster outlets (located in GI Joe stores or call 800-745-0888) sell Raz Transportation's economical bus/lift packages. Pickup is from GI Joe parking lots. EcoTours of Oregon (503-245-1428) customizes day trips including hotel pickup. The Alpental-Snoqualmie-Ski Acres-Hyak* mega-ski-opolis, all connected by single management and ski trail or shuttle bus, is less than fifty miles from Seattle. The I-90 Express (206-434-7669, extension 3242) operates on Saturdays from five pickup points in and around Seattle.

Across the border, Grouse Mountain* is just half an hour's drive from Vancouver. BC Transit (604-261-5100) runs public buses, or you can treat yourself to a Seatrain "cruise" from downtown. An inexpensive all-day public-transportation pass for all buses, Seatrain and the Skybus monorail is an excellent value. Vancouverites ski mighty Whistler and Blackcomb, seventy miles and under two hours from the city, as a daytrip all the time, and so can you. Maverick Coach Lines (604-662-8051) runs buses between the airport and downtown and the resort, while Perimeter Tours & Travel (604-266-5386) and Gray Lines (800-665-2122, 604-244-3744) provide just city-ski service.

Vacationers have additional choices for city-based skiing. Burlington, Vermont, is within an hour's drive of Bolton Valley, Jay Peak, Smugglers' Notch, Stowe and Sugarbush. In the past, packages combining Burlington accommodations and lift-ticket vouchers have existed, and they might return. Northern Vermont is within reasonable driving distance of the vast population belt that stretches from the Middle Atlantic States to coastal New England. If you fly, you'll have to factor in the cost of a rental car. Other cities offer convenient access to one ski area, and lift/lodging packages are often available. The most beguiling combination is Quebec City and Mont Ste.-Anne. Extremely well-priced packages in central British Columbia combine skiing at Silver Star with lodging in Vernon or skiing at Sun Peaks and lodging in Kamloops. Both are lively small cities with abundant economy accommodations, well-priced restaurants and colleges, which guarantee the presence of nightspots and other evening entertainment. You can also couple lodging in Bozeman, Montana, and skiing Bridger Bowl (or even Big Sky); Missoula and Montana Snowbowl; Boise and Bogus Basin; Santa Fe and Ski Santa Fe; and Grand Junction, Colorado, and Powderhorn.

...OR IN A NEIGHBORING TOWN Sometimes a neighboring town rather than a city provides the economical lodging alternative to a pricier resort. Colorado offers several such options. If you want to ski Vail and Beaver Creek, lodging will cost less in Avon, or if Summit County is your destination, lodging in Dillon, Frisco or Silverthorne is less. Free buses connect these towns with their more glamorous neighbors. Glenwood Springs is a feasible commute from Aspen, with low-cost RAFTA bus service between them and the possibility of going to Ski Sunlight for part of your vacation. Moderately priced lodging is also popping up along Route 82 between Aspen and Glenwood in such towns as Basalt, El Jebel and Carbondale. The Ski Telluride Half-Price program institutionalizes such savings by coupling lodging in towns twenty-one or more miles from the resort with skiing at Telluride. There's no organized transportation option, so this package isn't for fainthearted winter drivers, but you can buy a good set of studded snow tires for the money you save.

The nearby town may be a summer resort with ample, winterized lodging, such as Lake George, New York, near Gore Mountain; Rangeley, Maine, near Saddleback; Gettysburg, Pennsylvania, near Ski Liberty; Hood River, Oregon, near the Mt. Hood ski areas; and Salida and Buena Vista, Colorado, near Monarch. Occasionally, the "nearby town" is also the one with the closest airport. Great packages combine accommodations in Durango with skiing at Purgatory. A skier shuttle connects the two, so you won't need a car. If you are skiing Crested Butte, you can stay in Gunnison, which, like Durango, has a batch of budget motels as well as other accommodations, but you will need wheels.

TIME YOUR TRAVEL

If you can't ski any time other than the Christmas-New Year's holidays, expect to pay top dollar and endure maximum crowds everywhere from liftlines to restrooms. The second most expensive time in the East and Midwest is during President's Week; at destination resorts in the West, it is President's Week through late March. One of the easiest ways to economize on your ski vacation is to take it any time except those periods.

Looking at it from the other perspective, rates are at their rock-bottom lowest between Thanksgiving and Christmas and again at the very end of the season. The next lowest rates are during the January off-peak period.

Early- and late-season skiing naturally carries inherent risks, the main gamble, of course, being on snow, which is why prices are so low. Conditions may be dicey, but in years when snow falls early or lingers late, you may reap the best skiing for the least money. Another benefit of early-season skiing is that free lodging deals and learn-to-ski incentives are clustered at that time. A benefit of late-season vacationing is that the weather is benign, the parties crank into high gear and spring corn snow is just plain fun to ski. Late season in the East and Midwest is generally anything from mid to late March on. In the West, March and April generally bring the season's heaviest snowfalls, and spring skiing starts in April. If you are quite flexible and want to wait until the last minute, you can usually find a last-minute place in a resort that is not full at these times.

Virtually every resort in the land offers some kind of off-season pricing. For instance, Crested Butte's groundbreaking Ski Free offer (see "Ticket Tactics," page 10) makes for budget vacationing, as do its imitators sprinkled throughout ski country. Park City's Toucan promotion gives skiers one night of free lodging for every two nights purchased early and late in the season. Do that math. It means that on a six-night vacation, you'll just pay for four nights of lodging, lift tickets may be reduced as well and some restaurants and shops also drop their prices. In Colorado, two Summit County resorts make almost as good an offer. Guests booking a minimum of four nights' lodging and three days' skiing at Keystone or Breckenridge during certain nonholiday weeks get one additional night and one more day free. Timberline, West Virginia, not only offers great rates at the beginning and end of the ski season, but the fifth day of a midweek package is free too. During Breckenridge's Beach Daze, which runs throughout April, lodging properties drop their rates by as much as 40 percent, lift tickets are lowered and a number of bars and restaurants also put on specials. In the East and Midwest, the "January thaw" is common enough to have a cliché name, and in the West, days are short and often blustery. However, modern snowmaking enables ski areas to recover surprisingly quickly from the thaw, and western weather can also be benign in midwinter. Specials packages again abound.

In addition to seasonal price fluctuations, the days of the week can make a difference in prices. Areas that thrive on weekend business offer the sorts of astonishing bargains that the major Rocky Mountain destination areas simply don't. The quantity and variety of bargains stipulated for "nonholiday midweek" skiing are astonishing, and if you sneak away for five days in the East, Midwest or West coast, your pocketbook will barely be picked. Lodging properties in Western destination resorts often require seven-night packages, while those with the bulk of their traffic on weekends offer the best deals for five midweek days. Some also have excellent long-weekend rates to entice skiers to tack an extra couple of days onto their normal two days of skiing. Snowbird, Utah, promotes early-week packages. A three- to five-night stay must start on Sunday night, and airfare, ground transportation and lifts are included for one bargain rate. Still other resorts adjust their pricing according to the time in their guests' lives in addition to the time of season or time of week. Kids-free programs proliferate (see "Family Values," page 48), but good deals for seniors are around, too. Copper Mountain, Colorado, for instance, discounts nightly lodging rates by 20 percent for guests sixty or older on packages booked within thirty days of arrival.

Conventional wisdom dictates making reservations early, especially if you plan to travel and ski during peak holiday periods. It is true that you'll be more likely to get your pick of accommodations and first choice of dates if you book early, but don't let procrastination discourage you. Travelers constantly must cancel reservations for various personal or business reasons, and you may be able to slip into a recently vacated space. Sometimes bookings are slow because the economy is weak or weather patterns seem unfavorable. In cases like that, resorts sometimes offer super-specials in normally slow periods and even good deals during normal peaks if reservations soften or cancellations occur. The January 1995 meltdown of snow is a perfect example. A horrific thaw hit the Northeast and Midwest, spurring a flood of cancellations. But the weather quickly turned cold, and ski areas used their snowmaking might to recover quickly. Still, they had beds and lifts to fill, and a number of them floated great last-minute deals. The lesson is that if a good deal materializes and you are available, jump on it.

BUY AN INCLUSIVE PACKAGE

Old-time ski weeks that included accommodations, two meals a day, lift tickets, ski lessons and often some après-ski activities in the evening are, if not quite as extinct as dinosaurs, certainly endangered vacation species. You may succumb to sticker shock when you look at the numbers that follow the dollar sign in an inclusive package, but when you recover enough to tally up what you get, you may be surprised at the value as well as the predictability of the "all-in" package. When you compare the base prices of different packages, bargain rates usually buy the no-frills variety, and you'll be stacking up extras day by day. Be a wise consumer and do some serious comparison shopping, looking not just at the showcase number but at what a vacation is really likely to cost.

Taos Ski Valley, New Mexico, the last bastion of the traditional ski week, is a challenging ski area, where good skiers go year after year to get even better. Ski-Better-Weeks consist of six days of lifts and lessons and seven nights of lodging and meals at one of four charming owner-operated lodges at the base of the lifts. The price is not low, but the value is significant, especially during off-peak weeks. There are three price tiers: regular season during the Christmas holidays and from early February through late March; value season from New Year's until the first week of February; and supersaver season before Christmas and the last two weeks of the season—all for the budget-conscious skier.

The ski week has had a renaissance at Stowe, the northern Vermont resort that long positioned itself as "the ski capital of the East." The package of the 1990s includes five-and-a-half days of skiing (to accommodate Sunday afternoon arrivals), five nights of accommodations, five days of lessons and a coupon book for goods and services throughout the resort. In addition, one child per paying adult stays free. Several of the sessions have been designated as Kids' Carnival Weeks with an array of additional savings and activities for youngsters. Across the country, Sugar Bowl, California, like Stowe a resort that dates back half a century, has a five-night ski week with skiing, accommodations and breakfast and dinner included in the daily price.

If Taos has maintained the format and Stowe has revived it, Club Med (800-CLUB-MED) has perfected the concept of the all-inclusive vacation. Accommodations in hotels, which are referred to as "villages," lift tickets, three meals a day (including wine or beer with dinner), après-ski entertainment and children's programs are packaged at one price. The only extras are rental equipment and drinks, and there is no tipping. Club Med typically also has negotiated favorable airfares from most cities. The friendly, hospitable format provides a painless way to experiment with your first European ski vacation, and several "international villages" in France and Switzerland cater to English speakers. Club Med's only North American ski village is at Copper Mountain, Colorado.

A handful of other ski resorts, notably The Balsams/Wilderness, New Hampshire, and Sugarloaf, Maine, have also retained or revived the classic ski week. At The Balsams, "all-inclusive" extends to a choice of menu for breakfast and dinner prepared by the resort's award-winning chefs, unlimited Alpine and cross-country skiing and snowboarding, skating and nightly entertainment. The Mt. Airy Lodge, Pennsylvania, has midweek packages including accommodations, meals, lift tickets, skating and evening entertainment. Smugglers' Notch, Vermont, has its own version, with packages that are not quite on the order of Club Med's when it comes to how much is included. Still, their excellent family programs factor in many components that normally have to be purchased separately. Big Sky, Montana, offers four- and seven-night versions of what are still called Great Ski Weeks. Scheduled from opening until just before Christmas and again during approximately the last week of the ski season, they cover hotel or condominium lodging, daily breakfast, skiing and an assortment of evening activities. Children ten and under stay and ski free, and there's not even an add-on for their breakfasts.

Dude ranches' rates cover accommodations, hearty meals, entertainment and any on-site activities—including guided horseback rides, cross-country skiing and snowshoeing. Shuttle service to the nearest Alpine area is also part of the price, but lift tickets and other on-slope services are additional. Lone Mountain Ranch (406-995-4644) is on-campus at Big Sky, Montana. In addition to easy access to Alpine skiing, the ranch's cross-country trail system is exemplary. Among the Colorado guest ranches offering the opportunity to go Alpine skiing are Colorado's C Lazy U, The Home Ranch, Skyline Guest Ranch and Vista Verde Ranch. Latigo Ranch, Fryingpan River Ranch, Peaceful Valley Ranch and Whistling Acres, also in Colorado, offer cross-country skiing and snowshoeing but are more than an hour from the nearest Alpine skiing. For more information on ranches in the state that are open in winter, write or call the Colorado Dude and Guest Ranch Association, P.O. Box 300, Tabernash, CO 80478; (800) 441-6060.

THE COUPON CAPER

Did you file a claim in 1993 against airline price-fixing? Do you still have some AirScript coupons lying around? Did you eat the right peanut butter, accrue enough credits with your long-distance carrier, stack up enough frequent flyer miles or in any other way qualify for a coupon entitling you to free or discounted air travel? Car rentals? Hotel overnights? Did you accept a bump from an overbooked flight in exchange for a certificate good for a future round-trip? A ski vacation is a good time to use them. Winter restrictions, except during key holiday periods, are less severe than in the summer, so you might have a decent shot at getting the flights and other services you want. Your chances are increased if you are able to fly midweek. Some programs maintain wait lists to see if flights open up; others give priority to travelers who buy one ticket and use mileage credits for a second. Once you've gotten bonus airfare, you can try to extend your stay at your. destination, but major resorts may not be able to do that at crowded times. Alternatives would be to do some sight-seeing in the gateway city or add on a few days in a smaller town nearby with more midweek vacancies.

The Yellow Pages of Skiing (800-864-2SKI), a handy reference tool for contacting ski areas, hotels and other resort services, also has coupons for discounts on lift tickets, dining, lodging and activities in ski country. Visitors' guides issued by local chambers of commerce, convention and visitors' bureaus and state tourism promotion agencies often contain coupons too. You can plug general coupon books or discount cards into your ski vacation plans. Such programs, whose main purpose is filling undersold hotel rooms by discounts of up to 50 percent, based on availability, are accepted by some ski-resort properties. They are also useful if you plan to overnight in a gateway city before or after you go skiing. Leaf through your books for values on airline tickets, rental cars, meals and, in some cases, lift tickets and rentals. The biggest company is Entertainment Publications (800-445-4137). Among its dozens of regional versions, the Gold C Book marketed in the Front Range includes an entire section of discounts on accommodations, lifts, equipment rentals and dining at several top Colorado ski resorts. You can save enough on one hotel night to pay for the cost of the book.

If you are on certain real estate or phone sales mailing lists, you may be offered a free or discounted trip if you are willing to sit through a sales pitch for a time-share or condo. The Fairfield Pagosa Resort near Pagosa Springs and Wolf Creek Ski Area, Colorado, has been contacting potential buyers by direct mail for years. Now that other big-league property developers and managers such as Marriott are plunging into the resort timeshare business, you can expect more such marketing efforts. If you receive a solicitation implying that you may have won a free trip but need to pay some sort of processing fee, or anything else that smells of a scam, don't take the bait.

LOYALTY REWARDED

With the hot competition between credit card companies, notably American Express and Visa, special vacation deals are often available with the use of a specific credit card. American Express, for instance, has an ongoing promotion with Snowbird, offering lift-lodging packages at up to 45 percent off peak-season prices and a three-nighter at Bromley, Vermont, with a great value for early-week lodging, skiing, dining and shopping. "Telluride Ski Mountain" has starred in Visa's TV commercials, which offer

MULTI-AREA TICKETS

We all like to get value for our money, and multi-area tickets and coupon books give us just that. When you are vacationing, they enable you to sample several ski areas from one lodging base. The variety puts extra sparkle in a ski trip—and sometimes, it gives you ideas for future travels.

SKI AREA	THE DEAL
Aspen Four Mountain Ticket	All tickets fully interchangeable at Aspen Highlands, Aspen Mountain, Buttermilk and Snowmass
Boyne Pass	Big Sky, MT; Boyne Mountain, Boyne Highlands, MI; Brighton, UT
Eastern Townships Big Five	5-day packages with skiing at Bromont, Mont Sutton, Orford and Owl's Head, QU, and Jay Peak, VT
Jackson Hole Ski Three	Interchangeable pass for Jackson Hole, Grand Targhee and Snow King, WY, with extra services at the two smaller mountains included
K-A-B	Fully interchangeable lift tickets at Keystone, Arapahoe Basin and Breckenridge, CO
LBO Tickets	Various interchangeable deals for Attitash/Bear Peak and Cranmore, NH; Sugarbush, VT; and Sunday River, ME, all operated by LBO Enterprises
Lake Louise/Nakiska/Fortress Mountain, AB	A Lake Louise lift pass is accepted at Nakiska and Fortress Mountain, AB. A Nakiska/Fortress Mountain ticket is totally interchangeable.
Mammoth-June Mountain	Interchangeable lift tickets
Okemo-Stratton Ticket	Okemo and Stratton, VT; reciprocal skiing on 3-day or longer ticket
The Pass, WA	All lift tickets valid at Alpental, Snoqualmie, Ski Acres and Hyak, and it is possible to ski between several of these areas
Peaks of Excitement	Various interchangeable deals for Killington, Mt. Snow/Haystack and sometimes Bromley, VT; Sugarloaf, ME; and Waterville, NH

Ski Club Banff	Multiday plans for Lake Louise, Norquay/Mystic Ridge and Sunshine Village, AB
Ski Lake Tahoe	Alpine Meadows, Heavenly Ski Resort, Northstar-at-Tahoe, Sierra-at-Tahoe and Squaw Valley USA skiable on voucher books for several lengths
Ski New Hampshire Family Pass	Coupon book for 5 consecutive days of midweek skiing at all New Hampshire ski areas except Wildcat; 1 children's book free with every adult purchase
Ski Over the Mountains	Multiday ticket holders may ski over Stowe's Big Spruce or Smugglers' Notch's Sterling Mountain and ride the other resort's lift for a small upgrade fee
Ski Tahoe North	Interchangeable lift tickets valid at 12 Alpine and 7 cross-country areas
Ski Utah	5-out-of-6- and 6-out-of-7-day voucher books for skiing at Alta, Brighton, Deer Valley, Park City, Solitude, Snowbird, Sundance or Wolf Mountain
Ski Vermont's Classics	Multiday pass for Jay Peak, Smugglers' Notch, Sugarbush and Stowe (program specifics have changed frequently)
Snowshoe/SilverCreek	Fully interchangeable tickets at these 2 nearly adjacent West Virginia resorts
Vail/Beaver Creek	All tickets fully interchangeable at these 2 Colorado ski areas (includes Arrowhead until it is merged into Beaver Creek)
Whistler	Fully interchangeable multiday ticket good at Blackcomb and Whistler Mountain

Just as this book was going to press, LBO Enterprises (Sunday River, Maine; Attitash/Bear Peak and Cranmore, New Hampshire; and Sugarbush, Vermont) announced the acquisition of S-K-I Ltd. (Killington and Mt. Snow/Haystack, Vermont; Sugarloaf/USA, Maine and Waterville Valley, New Hampshire). It is reasonable to assume that various joint marketing efforts and additional skier values will ensue in future seasons.

special discount plans. In both cases, packages must be charged on the appropriate card. The Aspen Skiing Company and the Keystone/Brecken-ridge/Arapahoe Basin complex are among the resorts that have sent past patrons gift certificates good for future savings on lift tickets, ski school, rental shops and various lodges in Aspen and Snowmass.

SMART STRATEGIES FOR SPECIAL SITUATIONS

Some ways of saving money or getting the most for your skiing dollar are all-purpose, one-size-fits-all, but others fit specific skiers' needs. In addition to ideas from other chapters, like joining a ski club (see "The Group," page 119), obtaining the best buy for your family's ski vacation (see "Family Values," page 48) or specifically saving on accommodations (see "Sleep Cheap," page 90), you can use some hints for your particular situation.

BEATING THE SINGLE SUPPLEMENT

Ever since Captain Noah penalized singles on the Ark, travel has been two by two. "Single supplement" is travelese for the surcharge levied against single travelers above the standard per-person, double occupancy rate divided by two. For solo travelers, the phrase "per person, double occupancy" therefore holds particular dread. It means that an individual pays far more than half a twosome for accommodations and even entire vacation packages. In fact, one of the reasons for Club Med's early success and popularity with singles is that the club didn't discriminate financially or socially against those who vacation alone.

Some enlightened ski resorts periodically offer well-priced packages for singles. The format for these good values varies slightly, and packages are often offered only on a space-available basis, so don't expect them at Christmas or President's Weekends or any other time that lodging demand is high. Copper Mountain, Colorado; Killington, Vermont; and Northstar-at-Tahoe, California, have led the charge with packages aimed at singles including well-priced lodging, lift tickets and various extras. Sun Valley, Idaho, goes all out for singles with an annual It Happened at Sun Valley week, generally in mid-January. It features seven nights' lodging, a five-out-of-six-day lift ticket and all sorts of social events unabashedly aimed at helping single skiers overcome that state—and perhaps return as couples the following year.

Several match-up services that find travel partners may also include skiers seeking other skiers. These services generally charge a membership fee, which easily pays for itself if you find someone with whom to double up. Some services are outdoors- and sports-oriented dating services, while others offer the option of same- or opposite-sex traveling companions, with or without the romance component. The Travel Companion Exchange (P.O. Box 833, Amityville, NY 11701-0833; 516-454-0880) will take your quest to more than 6,000 singles nationally. The fee is less for people seeking same-sex travel partners, more for those who wish to be matched up with the opposite sex. TCE is one of the most established such services. Its bimonthly newsletter features personal-ad-type listings from single, widowed and divorced people seeking a companion or just wanting travel tips. Enterprising singles can also embark on their own search where resorts, packagers and services haven't done so. Local personals ads or national singles-matching services are among the routes to consider—of course, taking all precautions you would in partnering up with a stranger.

Just as adult travel has traditionally been on a PPDO basis, family travel is usually geared to a pair of parents and their child(ren). For information on places where single parents (and grandparents) get a break on a ski vacation, see the "Family Values" chapter.

TAKE A TAX-DEDUCTIBLE SKI BREAK

Unless the tax code is rewritten once again, professional seminars, even at resorts, still meet Internal Revenue Service requirements for tax deductibility. Programs for physicians, dentists, attorneys and accountants are the most common. Some professional groups organize seminars directly with ski resorts, and the American Educational Institute (800-354-3507) produces seminars at selected Colorado resorts. They comply with current tax laws and are approved for continuing education credits to qualified professionals.

SPRING BREAK AND OTHER ESCAPES FROM EDUCATION

When it comes to luring college students, Killington, Vermont, calls itself the "University of Diversity" and likens its six-summit ski area to a "campus" and skiing to "attending class." All this is a clever way of promoting its Collegiate Ski Fest Weeks, which in truth are great, fun-filled deals for students. Offered since 1979, these midweek packages are available just before and after Christmas and at semester break time in late January. They include lodging, lift tickets and a full curriculum of après-ski events, plus a card good for additional discounts at shops, restaurants and clubs around the mountain. Sunday River, Maine, produces Gotta Rock Ski Weeks in January, with special discounts for college students and a variety of day and night diversions. Waterville Valley College Weeks, staged during a couple key weeks in January, include skiing, lodging, health-club admission and an array of organized competitions in everything from broomball and Walleyball to snowboarding and skiing. Steamboat's College Ski Weeks are on the docket the first half of January.

SKI THE GREAT WHITE NORTH

Canadian resorts are a lot like their U.S. counterparts, just a little colder and a lot cheaper. No matter how you cut it, Canadian skiing is a bargain for Americans. For the last several years, the Canadian dollar has been worth at least one-third less than U.S. currency. That makes for an automatic and very substantial "discount" on every ski vacation—holiday and nonholiday, low season and high season, large resort and small. With the open-skies policies agreed to in 1995 by the American and Canadian governments, air service is improving and fares should be competitive.

Since the majority of Canada's population lives within a hundred miles of the U.S. border, most of the country's ski areas are also in the southern part of our northern neighbor. This puts them within vacation driving range of many Americans too. Skier patterns largely reflect those in the U.S. as well. Eastern areas tend to attract weekenders and therefore offer the best midweek bargains, while large western ones are destination resorts with a hefty midweek business overlaid with daytrippers and weekend skiers from such cities as Vancouver and Calgary.

Canadians have a lot of winter, and they've learned to love it. More than 150 ski areas dot the vast landscape, from White Hills overlooking the Atlantic Ocean from Newfoundland's rocky heights to Mt. Washington on British Columbia's Vancouver Island on the Pacific. Among them are small local hills and noteworthy destination resorts. In western Canada, Whistler Village, gateway to Blackcomb and Whistler, the two North American mountains with the highest and second-highest verticals, consistently tops the charts for great skiing on this continent. The three ski areas around Banff (Lake Louise, Sunshine and Norquay/Mystic Ridge) combine great skiing on one lift pass, fabulous scenery and a nifty town. Sun Peaks is an up-and-comer, with fabulous skiing and a nascent village. One of skiing's classic eastern areas, Tremblant, has undergone a true renaissance and now has state-of-the-art on-mountain facilities and a fine new village that turns a classic ski mountain into a terrific resort. Tremblant today combines the kinds of up-to-date facilities that $200 million could buy with Québeçois atmosphere. Mont Ste.-Anne combines stateside convenience with French charm. Skiers can choose between staying and playing at the resort or in Quebec City, half an hour away.

The Canadian Rockies' major ski meccas offer two-for-one values to U.S. skiers. In addition to the favorable exchange rate, winter is off-season in such resort towns as Banff, Jasper and Lake Louise. All accommodations, but particularly those in Jasper, slash their rates during ski season. Even the grand hotels operated by the CP Hotels (800-441-1414) chain—the Banff Springs Hotel, Chateau Lake Louise and Jasper Park Lodge—are affordable. These luxurious hotels, which are nearly impossible to book in the summer, welcome skiers and even offer well-priced packages, including shuttle buses to the lifts and extras summer guests can only dream about.

The best inclusive ski weeks may still be found north of the border as well. Gray Rocks, a fabled ski lodge and ski hill in the Laurentians north of Montreal, is the last bastion of the traditional ski week. Accommodations, meals, lifts, ski instruction, a variety of extras and even gratuities are all wrapped into one base price. Nearby Club Tremblant packages five nights of lodging, five days of skiing, daily breakfasts, dinners and pack lunches, ski instruction, shuttle to Mont Tremblant's lifts and use of the sports center.

For Canadian skiers, of course, the exchange rate is unfavorable. Therefore, when they ski south of their border, ski areas such as Jay Peak, Vermont, and Schweitzer Mountain, Idaho, which have accepted Canadian currency at par, are considered values.

HOW TO AFFORD THAT EUROPEAN DREAM

For skiers, the Alps are like Mecca is to Moslems. They are the mountain range where skiing and ski vacationing as we know them developed. For Americans, a winter trip there is two vacations in one: a ski vacation and a trip to Europe. With the weakness of the American dollar against major European currencies, it also has a reputation for being unaffordable, so many skiers view it as an impossible dream. For East Coast skiers who plan wisely, pick a package carefully and are willing to forego the most luxurious accommodations, the total cost for Europe can be quite similar to the total cost for the Rockies. Joining a ski club trip or booking through a tour operator is a good way to take a value vacation. Group savings are even more vital than for a domestic vacation because that's the only predictable way to snare a good airfare. (Even if you use your frequent flyer miles to get to Europe, you might be able to hook onto an organized program by purchasing a "land only" package.) From the Midwest and

West, the Alps are more expensive than the Rockies or the Sierra, and it is even more important to cut the best deal you can.

Of the four major Alpine countries, you can expect to find the lowest prices in Italy, midrange packages to Austria and France and the most expensive skiing and lodging in Switzerland. In addition, some adventurous skiing travelers explore resorts in Slovenia and even Bulgaria. Prices are modest, but facilities and infrastructure are rarely up to mainline Alpine standards.

European and western ski vacations don't necessarily come in at vastly different total prices because typical packages are structured differently. When you buy a package to a U.S. resort, the price generally includes airfare, lodging and lift tickets. Ground transportation is often an add-on, and local taxes are also normally extra. Most European ski packages include airfare, ground transfers and lodging. Lift passes are generally additional. But this isn't as bad as it seems. Without the onerous liability laws that inflate the cost of U.S. lift tickets, the price of skiing itself is surprisingly low. In many Alpine resorts you can ski literally dozens of lifts, including those in neighboring towns, on a fully interchangeable ticket. In addition, many European inns and hotels include breakfast and often dinner in their prices, and taxes and service charges are also included in package prices.

Some of the specific strategies that work for stateside ski vacations also work for the Alps. For instance, you can pick a small town near a major resort, and with Europe's wide-ranging network of interconnected ski lifts and runs, you can usually ski from your village. In Austria, these would include Stuben near St. Anton and Kirchberg near Kitzbühel. In France, you can stay for less in Tignes than in Val d'Isère, Morzine than Avoriaz, or Bourg St.-Maurice than Les Arcs. You can go to a Club Med, which has numerous ski villages in France and Switzerland. You can stay in a vibrant city like Innsbruck or Salzburg, Austria, or Interlaken, Switzerland, and ski a different nearby area every day, with bus transfer included in the package price.

Other European policies ease budget-skiing in Europe. Every country has its own rating system, with specific standards for accommodations in various categories from one to four or five stars. It's easy to know roughly what you'll get for your money, even when the lodging is in a small village several thousand miles from home, just by the way it's rated. U.S. tour operators have adopted these ratings and use them in their literature. Additionally, Europe can be an affordable family vacation, and an educational one as well. In most European countries, children's lift rates extend to about age sixteen, and family or children's rates are common in hotels.

Except in modern French resorts, condominiums are less pervasive than in North America, meaning that you and your children will have contact with an international cadre of skiers.

Finally, the differential between high and low season is far greater than here—and seasonality applies not just to lodging but to lift passes as well. Since Europe has no Thanksgiving, the ski season officially begins at Christmas. Rates before the holidays are rock-bottom, while those around the Christmas-New Year's period are sky-high. January and early February are good for budget-watchers, while late February and March are again high season. As in the U.S., late-season rates drop again.

For further information on European skiing, contact:

Austrian National Tourist Office	P.O. Box 1142, New York, NY 10108, (212) 944-6880
Bulgarian Tourist Information Center	317 Madison Ave., New York, NY 10017, (212) 573-5530
French Government Tourist Office	444 Madison Ave., New York, NY 10011, (900) 990-0040 ($.50 a minute)
Italian Government Tourist Board	630 Fifth Ave., New York, NY 10111, (212) 245-4822
Slovenian Tourist Office	122 East 42nd St., New York, NY 10168, (212) 682-5896
Switzerland Tourism	608 Fifth Ave., New York, NY 10020, (212) 757-5944

THE BOTTOM LINE

You may not consider either Aspen, Colorado, or Austria's St. Anton as bargain destinations, nor would you necessarily slot a high-season trip to either destination into your plans for economy skiing. Still, the Austrian National Tourist Office's comparison between the total cost of a vacation from New York to these two glamorous resort areas is instructive in weighing costs. Obviously, any vacation on either continent costs less in low season or if you select moderately priced lodging, and there are more economical resort regions than these two, but here's how the two stacked up for a February 1996 ski vacation:

RESORT	ASPEN	ST. ANTON
Package price	$1,127	$1,450
Airfare from New York	Included	Included
International departure tax	Not applicable	$35 to $45
Transfers	Hotel provides or additional	Included
Accommodations in first-class hotel	Included	Included
Breakfast and dinner	Additional (ANTO estimates $350)	Included
Six-day lift pass	Included	$198
Local taxes	Included	Included
Service charges	Additional	Included

SNOWCAT SKIING

Arguably the most extravagant ski vacation is a heli-skiing trip, but it is also the dream trip wrapped in visions of untracked powder. Snowcat skiing is the budget version. It's a lot like heli-skiing without the chopper. Both conveyances ferry small groups of a dozen or fewer lucky skiers and snowboarders beyond ski area boundaries. Equipped with avalanche transceivers and accompanied by one or usually two guides, they experience skiing conditions as nature meant them to be—no snowmaking, no grooming, no lifts in sight. In addition to cost, the major advantage of cats over copters is that vehicles aren't grounded by weather. The downside is that you can't ski around as vast a region as in a helicopter. Verticals, snack and lunch breaks and format are similar. Most snowcat operations are by the day (some with half-day or overnight options), including use of avalanche transceivers and usually lunch. Fat skis, available for rent, are recommended for maximum control and pleasure in powder or chop. Lift tickets are sometimes extra. Reservations, of course, are mandatory except at selected operations in ski areas' future expansion terrain.

UNITED STATES

COLORADO   Aspen Powder Tours' (800-525-6200, 970-925-1227) is the Cadillac of snowcat ski tours with bowl and glade skiing on 1,500 acres off the back side of Aspen Mountain. Groups average ten 1,000-vertical-foot trips a day skiing pitches of 20 to 30 degrees. The program includes a gourmet lunch catered by the posh Little Nell Hotel and served in a mountain cabin.

Though Chicago Ridge isn't adjacent to Ski Cooper (719-486-2277), this smallish ski area, an easy day hop from Vail or Summit County, runs snowcats in one of the Rockies' biggest permit areas—1,800 acres of bowls and glades. Full- and half-day tours are offered.

Great Divide Snow Tours are available at Monarch (719-539-3573, ext. 116), one of Colorado's renowned powder areas. The skiing is on six hundred acres of open slopes, chutes and glades off the Beezeway chair. Full-day (including lunch), half-day and single-run options are offered at a moderate price.

Irwin Lodge, a pristine resort twelve miles from Crested Butte, operates North America's largest powder-skiing operation with seven snowcats on 2,400 acres with a maximum vertical of 2,100 feet. Day trips and overnight packages are available with accommodations and meals in a twenty-three-room log lodge. Cost is reasonable and, on day trips, includes transportation from Crested Butte and lunch.

Snowmass (800-525-6200) offers free snowcat tours to the Cirque, where intermediates can ski a groomed run and experts can tackle some true extreme terrain. The capacity is ten groups of fourteen skiers per day. You must register at Up 4 Pizza the day you wish to take the tour.

Steamboat Powder Cats (800-288-0543, 303-879-5188) groups average ten 1,000-vertical-foot runs a day. One snowcat (a new turbo-diesel) motors around on fifteen square miles of terrain, meaning that you're very likely to ski powder. The company offers something that most companies don't. Free powder lessons are included on the theory that getting all skiers up to speed is in everyone's best interest. An overnight option includes a stay in a rustic cabin with dorm accommodations for up to twelve people. The full-day program includes van transport from Steamboat; and the overnight trip includes three meals.

IDAHO Brundage Snow Cat (800-888-7544, 208-634-4151) tours feature 800- to 1,000-vertical-foot runs on Sargent's Peak, just north of the lift-served area. Groups warm up on gentle snowfields and progress to more challenging terrain. At this writing, the Forest Service is studying Brundage's application to expand to Granite Peak and/or Slab Butte one valley over, offering longer (to 2,000 vertical feet) and steeper (to 50 degrees) runs.

MONTANA Lone Mountain Ranch (406-995-4644) at Big Sky operates a snowcat into Moonlight Basin. With skiing on 25,000 private acres, there's now lone skiing on the back side of Lone Mountain. The vertical is nearly 1,700 feet—the top part with a relatively mellow 25-degree slope, the bottom with 35 degrees—with room for future expansion. Options include a day on the cat, or cat skiing plus meals and a night in a new yurt. Yurts, inspired by the tent-like structures used by nomadic Mongolians, have become popular backcountry shelters.

Sno-Cat Skiing at The Big Mountain (800-858-5493, 406-862-3511) is offered in the Caribou and Flower Point areas, slated for future lift service. In addition to the sort of sweeping terrain that characterizes north-ern Montana, the snowcat area offers fabulous views of Glacier National Park to the east. The cost is among the lowest of all cat tours.

NEW MEXICO   Ski Rio (505-758-7707) plans to offer snowcat skiing on Carmello Peak until a lift is installed in this as a future expansion area. Initially, six advanced and expert trails were cut on a 1,350-foot vertical. Unlimited snowcat runs are available for one modest surcharge above the cost of a lift ticket.

OREGON   Mount Bailey Snowcat Skiing's (800-733-7593, 503-793-3333) clients get in up to twelve runs a day with a maximum 3,000-foot vertical on a peak in central Oregon. Day skiing and multiday packages with accommodations and meals at the nearby Diamond Lake Lodge are available.

UTAH   Brian Head (800-272-7426, 801-677-2035) operates a snowcat service for advanced and expert skiers on 700 vertical feet of steep open bowls and steeper chutes. Skiers first ride the Giant Steps chairlift to 10,900 feet, and then the snowcat another 400, for Utah's highest skiing. Re-entry to the groomed terrain is about two-thirds of the way down the lift-served area. There is a very small per-ride charge in addition to the lift ticket.

At Deer Valley (800-424-DEER), hourly tours into a bowl slated for future expansion are given Wednesdays through Sundays for five dollars per hour in addition to a lift ticket. The vertical is 1,220 feet, and the terrain demands at least advance skiing ability. Park City Snow Cat Cruises (801-524-0214) picks skiers up from Deer Valley and takes them to Thou-sand Peaks Ranch, forty-five minutes from Park City. The terrain is inter-mediate to advanced, with per-run verticals of 1,300 to 3,200 feet. The cost is on the upper end, but offers such enhanced services as TV monitors in the snowcat cabins so skiers can watch videotapes of their runs on the ride up. The company also offers Ladies' Days on Mondays with 10 percent off, and provides optional half-day powder lessons at an additional fee. For non-powderhounds, there are also sight-seeing "cruises."

WYOMING   Targhee's Powder Cats operate out of Grand Targhee (800-443-8146, 307-353-2304), a vest-pocket resort on the Wyoming-

Idaho border. For resort guests, this is real no-fuss snowcat skiing. The cat heads for 1,500 acres on Peaked Peak right from the base area. The per-run vertical is 1,800 to 2,500 feet. Moderately priced full- and half-day tours are available.

CANADA

If you're heading north of the border, you can check out the following snowcat operations, which like all travel to Canada carry the automatic exchange-rate "discount": Cat Powder Skiing, Revelstoke, British Columbia (604-837-9489); Great Northern Snow-Cat Skiing, Calgary, Alberta (403-287-2267); Island Lake Mountain Tours, Fernie, British Columbia (604-423-3700); Lemon Creek Snowcat Skiing, Slocan, British Columbia (604-355-2403); Selkirk Wilderness Skiing, Meadow Creek, British Columbia (604-366-4424).

TURN A SKI VACATION INTO A WINTER VACATION

When you weekend-ski, you might be an absolute maniac, determined to wrest every last vertical foot out of your skiing day. You'll probably take a little of that approach on your vacation with you. But you might want to pull back, relax and explore some of winter's other pleasures. Most multiday lift tickets are for four-out-of-five, five-out-of-six or six-out-of-seven consecutive days of skiing. That leaves you with a day off to explore the resort, sight-see in the region and perhaps try other activities.

Two Colorado resorts make it easy to sample off-slope options. Purgatory's Total Ticket allows you to turn in any voucher on a four-day or longer package for a lift ticket, cross-country skiing, a ride on the fabled Durango & Silverton Narrow Gauge Railroad, a trip to Mesa Verde National Park, snowmobiling, a day at the Trimble Hot Springs including a massage or an excursion to the Sky Ute Casino. Vail's Mountain Plus Ticket similarly is good for skiing, snowmobiling, cross-country or snow-shoeing lessons, rentals or tours. These options are offered without major preplanning or financial penalty.

Even if your resort doesn't make it quite so easy, you'll most likely turn a great ski vacation into a totally memorable one if you sample some of the many available off-slope options. At the very least, visit the health club, take a leisurely dip in a swimming pool or do a few hours of cross-country skiing or snowshoeing into the surrounding countryside. The experience is sure to add immeasurably to the value of your ski vacation.

CHAPTER SIX

SLEEP CHEAP

Whenit comes to vacation budgeting, many skiers prefer to save on sleeping arrangements so that they can spend more on skiing or entertainment. You can stray from mainline ski resorts (see "Hidden Treasures," page 112), stay in a city or town near the resort you want to ski (see "Stretching Your Ski-Vacation Dollar," page 60) or, under the theory that your surroundings don't matter quite as much when you're asleep, try some other tactics to cut the cost of lodging. The caveat here is that many of the economy options will merely save money. They might require a big trade-off in privacy and/or comfort, which may be all right for some skiers but is unacceptable for others.

PACK A CONDO

The easiest way to stick to a budget is by packing as many bodies into a condo as management allows. This is one technique that ski clubs use to offer trips at such low prices. You can do the same. A typical two-bedroom unit that "sleeps six" will probably have one room with a king-sized bed, one with twin beds and a sleep sofa or Murphy bed in the living area. If you need to accommodate eight, you'll find a "two-bedroom with loft" cheaper than a three-bedroom unit. To save more, look for a unit with fewer bathrooms than bedrooms, or perhaps an older one without such conveniences as a microwave or a dishwasher. With all those bodies, there should be enough hands for dishwashing and other chores.

When you are traveling with your children, a one-bedroom unit will usually suffice. The adults get the bedroom, and the kids get the couch. Be sure you snare one of the ubiquitous kids-stay-free deals (see "Family Values," page 48) so that three or four of you can sleep (and perhaps ski) for the price of two. Whether you are part of a group of friends or members of a family, a condominium—even a full one—gives you some elbow room and, best of all for the budget, the chance to prepare your own breakfast, snacks and even dinner. If it's a ski-in, ski-out unit, you may even be able to pop in for a quick lunch with no lines and no daily cash outlay.

A number of factors influence the price you'll pay. The very most expensive will be a large, luxurious townhome-style condo, perhaps with a private, heated garage and at least one spacious bathroom for each bedroom, located slopeside in an expensive resort and rented in high season. Amenities might include a private hot tub, a wine cellar and designer furnishings. You'll live like royalty, but you'll pay dearly. Every one of those features that you're willing to scale down or trade off will save you money. A smaller, simpler unit with outdoor parking, located a distance from the mountain and rented during off-season will be economical.

Enterprising and energetic condo owners occasionally rent their units out independently, perhaps placing classified ads to attract renters (see "Shop the Classifieds," below). More commonly, condominiums will be a lodging option in ski packages booked through a tour operator. If you want to do further research or want more numbers to compare package prices, you can call central reservations at the resort you are considering or directly contact the management companies that are responsible for units as the owners' representative. You can also book your vacation through any of these sources, but if you do it through the central-reservations service, you are more likely to be able to find a package with airfare, lifts and other extras. You can also book a unit through a national service such as Condolink (800-733-4445), which handles both snowbelt and sunbelt locations.

SHOP THE CLASSIFIEDS

Classified ads in ski-town newspapers and major papers in big cities near ski country such as Denver, Boston or San Francisco can often point you to a well-priced condo. Tucked among the ads for national condo and time-share rental agencies and resort reservations services, you might find some ads inserted by locals who own and manage a condominium unit or two in a nearby ski resort. Because they handle all the details themselves, they do not pay a management fee, and the savings are often passed on to skiers. Sometimes ads are run by skiers who needed to cancel their vacations and would otherwise have to forfeit their deposits. In either case, you will be dealing with an individual, not an official management company or rental agency, which you can only do if you have the confidence to send a large check to a total stranger.

SKI-HOUSE SHARES

If you ski weekend after weekend, perhaps with a vacation week thrown in, nothing can beat the per-night savings involved in a ski-house share. Combine it with a season pass, preferably purchased early, and you can do a lot of skiing for very little money. Popular with urban singles, the format is pretty standard. Someone with responsibility, initiative and a penchant for savings rents a house for the season and puts out the word that shares are sought. Word-of-mouth, contact with previous sharers, classified ads in newspapers and postings on ski-hop bulletin boards are the best places to find openings in ski houses.

Half-shares (every other weekend) and full shares (every weekend) are usually offered. Weeknights are usually open for all on a first-come, first-served basis. Members generally pay the organizer in advance for the whole season and meet in the city to lay down ground rules. Commonly, sharers carpool from the city, agree on how to handle meals (paid for and cooked communally, eat breakfast in and members' choice for dinner, everyone on his or her own or whatever), cleaning, quiet hours and other policies.

Since organizers do the bulk of the work and take on the financial burden of deposits, deal with the property owner and organize the utilities, they usually sleep free all winter long. After you've been a member of a shared ski house, you may want to save big by taking on the task in the future.

In addition to all the other benefits, houses provide a built-in social circle. Sharers often dine and party together, and sometimes the party spreads to other groups. Killington annually runs a ski-house challenge, with prizes for the best racers and the best costumes. Jay Peak puts on a splendid Shack Race, using the popular Canadian term for ski house.

TIME-SHARES

If you can invest in more than just a season's worth of lodging, consider a time-share or interval ownership. It's a way of making a relatively small real estate investment that guarantees you a place to stay on your ski vacations for years to come. Rather than buying an entire condominium, you buy a share. A developer normally builds and furnishes a resort property and makes his or her initial profit by selling fifty weeks out of the year (the two remaining weeks are set aside for heavy cleaning and maintenance). If you buy, your share is priced according to which weeks are yours. Most units sleep four to six people and are therefore suitable for long-range vacationing.

Two advantages involve costs. Since you don't own the unit or its furnishings but are a shareholder, you don't have to pay for maintenance, repairs or replacement. If the snow is poor or the economy sours, you don't have to carry the cost if it isn't rented when you are not using it. On the other hand, the potential for increased profits is less than for a condominium, but that is not a factor if you are thinking of it as prepaid vacation accommodations rather than as an investment. It is best to look at them that way because time-share resales have a checkered history. Again to turn a disadvantage for someone else into an advantage for yourself, you may be able to pick up a resale at a very attractive price. For basic information on interval ownership, contact the American Resort Development Association, 1220 L Street NW, Washington, DC 20005; (202) 371-6700.

Another plus to time-shares is that you can use your weeks or swap them for comparable weeks at other resorts all over the country—and all over the world. That way, you won't be sentenced to twenty winters of skiing the same slopes if you prefer to explore other resorts. Two major time-share exchange organizations are Resort Condominiums International (317-871-9500) and Interval International (305-666-1861).

WINTER DEALS AT SUMMER RESORTS
Dozens of popular resorts where summer is high season are located within an hour's drive of top ski resorts. Management has decided it's more efficient to stay open year-round than to close and reopen annually, and good staff members are easier to keep if they have year-round employment. Usually it's skiers who have to make trade-offs to save money, but in this case, the resorts have done so by setting low winter rates. These properties are not inexpensive even in their off-season, but they float attractively priced packages and offer extras such as free shuttle to the slopes that make for excellent values.

Golf resorts in ski country include Tamarron Resort (800-678-1000) near Purgatory, Colorado; Grouse Mountain Lodge (800-321-8822) near The Big Mountain, Montana; and the Coeur d'Alene Resort (800-826-2390) near Silver Mountain, Idaho. Other fine resorts in top summer destinations also come with astonishingly low prices and good packages during ski season. These include the Spring Creek Resort (800-443-6139) near Jackson Hole; The Equinox (800-362-4747) near Bromley and Stratton, Vermont; the Woodstock Inn (800-448-7900) near Suicide Six, Killington and Okemo, Vermont; The Balsams/Wilderness, New Hampshire (800-255-0600) with its own on-site ski area; and CP Hotels' (800-441-4141) Banff Springs Hotel, Chateau Lake Louise and Jasper Park Lodge, all in Canada. In high-style Santa Fe, practically every place is on sale in winter, including the elegant, highly honored Inn of the Governeurs (800-234-4534) and the Hotel St. Francis (800-529-5700). Dude ranches, with their great winter prices and instinctive outdoor orientation, also make an excellent winter option for those with a few bucks to spend but none to waste (see "Stretching Your Ski-Vacation Dollar," page 60).

HIGH LIVING AT LOW PRICES

If you don't want to ski an unknown area, prefer in-season excitement to slow-season value periods and don't feel like commuting to the slopes, you can find ways to economize even in some of the country's most expensive resorts. Just realize that what is an inexpensive property in a luxury resort is likely to be priced on a par with a pretty fancy place at a budget resort. For example, Aspen innkeepers who were distressed at the town's image as a playground only for the wealthy have teamed up to create moderately priced three- to five-day packages. Gems of Aspen includes overnights in small lodges and lift passes valid on Aspen Mountain, Aspen Highlands, Buttermilk and Snowmass. For details, call Aspen Central Reservations, (800) 290-1325. Bed & Breakfast Vail represents private homes and some small inns in the Vail Valley and other Colorado resorts. To request a brochure of types of accommodations, send two dollars to Bed & Breakfast Vail, P.O. Box 491, Vail, CO 81658. For more information, call (970) 949-1212, weekdays between October 15 and April 15.

THE ALLURE (AND ECONOMY) OF BED-AND-BREAKFAST INNS

The bed-and-breakfast cult has spread across the land. You may love the atmospheric accommodations, often in exquisitely restored historic buildings, home-cooked breakfast every day and a special brand of personalized hospitality that are the hallmarks of these intimate inns. You will also find a romantic, tranquil atmosphere and contact with owners or managers that many travelers consider priceless. With breakfast and often after-ski refreshments included, B&Bs, though usually not cheap, often present good values.

National or regional, bed-and-breakfast reservations services and resort central reservations services can book inns. Guidebooks and specialized newsletters provide you with information on size, location, private versus shared baths (the latter may result in additional savings), type of breakfast and individual inns' policies on children (small ones are normally discouraged), pets (generally prohibited) and smoking (usually "non").

Among the proliferation of guidebooks, a few stand out as especially useful for skiers. *Colorado Bed & Breakfast* by Marie T. Layton (Fulcrum Publishing, 350 Indiana Street, Golden, CO 80401, 800-992-2908) features descriptions and photos of fifty-three special inns and *Absolutely Every Bed & Breakfast in Colorado* by Toni Knapp (Rockrimmon Press, 110 Enterprise, Colorado Springs, CO 81908, 800-530-8047) is a strictly factual compendium of every B&B in the country's top skiing state. *Great Affordable Bed & Breakfast Getaways* (MarLor Press, 4304 Brigadoon Drive, St. Paul, MN 55126, 800-669-4908) is a 308-page guide to budget B&Bs in North America. Since many inns don't accept youngsters, *Family Bed & Breakfast and Country Inns of New England* (Columbia Publishing, P.O. Box 1674, Wheat Ridge, CO 80034), based on the travels of the authors and their two children, is helpful for parents seeking a B&B vacation. *The Complete Guide to Bed and Breakfasts, Inns and Guesthouses* by Pamela Lanier (Lanier Publishing International, P.O. Box 20467, Oakland, CA 94620) is a good overall source for B&Bs.

Bed-and-breakfasts usually are just that, but an "inn" may have similar quality of charm, plus the option of MAP pricing. The letters stand for "modified American plan," meaning that both breakfast and dinner are included in the room or package rate. It is often just a few dollars higher than the breakfast-only offer. The cost-saving advantage for some skiers is offset by dining in the same place every evening. Country inns with MAP options are most common in New England. Many offer nonholiday midweek discounts too.

MOTEL CHEAP

Budget motels are short on charm but long on savings. If you consider your lodgings as only a place to sleep, shower and change clothes, and extra space, services or atmosphere are irrelevant, a budget motel might be a smart choice. You'll find these motels in abundance in resort areas that also attract large numbers of summer tourists. They are virtually nonexistent in built-for-skiing resort developments that control growth and style— generally with as much of an eye toward sales of high-priced real estate as toward sheer aesthetics. Budget motels usually have simple rooms, often basically furnished and small, functional bathrooms. Room doors often open directly from the outside, and soundproofing can be sparse. Amenities tend to be limited to such basics as soft-drink machines, an in-room coffeemaker and, with luck, a hot tub. Swimming pools are common, but they are usually not heated for the winter.

DORMEZ-VOUS

Dorms and bunkrooms were once as much a part of the American skiing tradition as T-bars and rope tows. They have largely gone out of style, but budget-watchers hope they will never become extinct. For the young (or the young at heart) on a budget, this is the way to go.

Most dorms separate men and women (though a handful are coed) in rooms sleeping from four to many more, usually in bunk beds. "Comforts" and "amenities" include shared baths, family-style meals, a telephone in the hall and a common area for après-ski. Some facilities are dorm-only; some have both regular and bunkrooms. Others have family bunkrooms sleeping four, six or perhaps eight; these are rented on a per-room rate with the greatest savings for a family or small group that puts a head on every pillow. Most supply linens (sometimes for a onetime fee), while others ask guests to bring their own linens or sleeping bags.

In most dorms and traditional lodges, nightlife tends toward games, puzzles, pool, table tennis, reading, TV and conversation around the fireplace. It's cheap too, as drinks are generally BYOB. There might be separate game and quiet rooms, perhaps a hot tub and occasionally even a swimming pool. When the dorm is part of a more upscale property, fancier facilities and more (also more expensive) après-ski options are at hand. In any case, with dorm accommodations, except for the family-room style, there are no single supplements, so the solo skier is not penalized. Prices usually include breakfast and often dinner, and when they do not, at least breakfast is usually offered at a small charge and guests have kitchen privileges. Some dorms also offer multiday discounts, lift-lodging packages and/or reduced rates for children. Most welcome groups with even lower per-person rates than the individual ones below. Especially in the East, dorms are rarely full on weeknights so that often, you will find even lower rates during nonholiday midweeks.

THE EAST

SKI AREA	THE DORM
Bretton Woods, NH	Crawford Hostel (603-466-2727)
	Iron Mountain House (603-383-9020)
Cranmore, NH	Cranmore Mountain Lodge (603-356-2044)
	Joe Dodge Lodge (603-466-2727)
Gunstock, NH	Cartway House (800-254-1172)
Jay Peak, VT	Greymour Ski Dorm (802-326-4794), also
	offers transportation from Amtrak station

Killington, VT	Alpenhof Lodge (800-SIX-MTNS) Fireside Lodge (802-422-3361) Turn of River Lodge (802-422-3766)
Mont Ste.-Anne, QU	Auberge du Fondeur (800-463-1568)
Mt. Sunapee, NH	Singing Hills (603-469-3236) Soo-Nipi Lodge (603-863-7509)
Mt. Washington Valley, NH (Attitash, Black Mountain, Cranmore, King Pine and Wildcat)	Applebrook (800-545-6504)
Okemo, VT	Trojan Horse* (802-228-5244)
Otis Ridge, MA	Grouse House (413-269-4446)
Ragged Mountain, NH	Owl's Nest (603-735-5159)
Stowe, VT	Round Hearth (802-253-7223) Siebeness Inn (800-426-9001) Spruce Peak Inn (802-253-4010), formerly Vermont State Ski Dorm
Stratton, VT	Vagabond Ski Lodge (802-874-4096)
Sugarloaf, ME	Sugarloafer's Ski Dorm (207-265-2041
Sunday River, ME	Chapman Inn (207-824-2657) Snow Cap Inn Ski Dorm (800-453-2SKI)
Whiteface/Lake Placid, NY	Adirondak Loj (518-523-3441) Cascade Cross-Country Center (518-523-9605) High Peaks Base Camp (518-946-2133)
Wildcat, NH	Appalachian Mountain Club (603-466-2727), with prices reduced for AMC members

THE WEST

SKI AREA	THE DORM
Alta, UT (dorms are not "cheap," but they offer substantial savings over the lodges' other room types)	Alta Lodge (800-748-5025) Alta Peruvian Lodge (800-453-8488) Goldminer's Daughter (800-453-4573) Rustler Lodge (800-451-5223) Snow Pine Lodge (801-742-2000)
Arizona Snowbowl, AZ	Weatherford Hotel (602-774-2731)
Aspen, CO	St. Moritz Lodge (970-925-3220)
Banff, AB	YWCA (403-762-3560)

Breckenridge, CO	The Fireside Inn* (970-453-6456)
Brighton, UT	Brighton Lodge (800-873-5512)
Crested Butte and Monarch, CO	Pitkin Hotel & Hostel* (970-641-2757), about 60 miles from these areas but very, very cheap
Eldora, CO	Boulder International Youth Hostel (303-442-9304)
Grand Targhee, WY	Teton Teepee (307-353-8176), located in Driggs, ID
Jackson Hole, WY	The Bunkhouse (307-733-3668) Hostel X* (307-733-3415)
Keystone, CO	Alpen Hütte Lodge* (970-468-6336), located in Silverthorne
Mammoth Mountain, CA	Hilton Creek International Hostel* (619-935-4989)
Montana Snowbowl, MT	BirchWood Hostel (406-728-9799)
Mt. Bachelor, OR	Bend Alpine Hostel (503-389-3813)
Mt. Hood Meadows, Mt. Hood Ski-bowl and Timberline, OR	Huckleberry Inn (503-272-3325)
Park City, UT	Chateau Après Lodge (801-649-9372) Dudler Dorms (800-453-5789)
Schweitzer, ID	Naples Hostel (208-267-2947), located in Naples
Silver Mountain ID	Kellogg International Youth Hostel* (208-783-4171)
Sipapu, NM	Sipapu Lodge & Dorm (505-587-2240), located near Valdito, 22 miles from Taos
Ski Sunlight, CO	Glenwood Springs Hostel * (970-945-8545), also with RAFTA bus access to Aspen and Snowmass
Snowbird, UT	Cliff Lodge (800-453-3000)
Squaw Valley, CA	Hostel at Squaw Valley (800-544-4723)
Taos, NM	Abominable Snow Mansion (505-776-8298)
Telluride, CO	Mountain View (970-882-7861), located in Dolores
Whistler/Blackcomb, BC	UBC Lodge (604-932-6604) Whistler Youth Hostel (604-932-5492)
Winter Park, CO	Winter Park Hostel* (970-726-5356)

These hostels belong to Hosteling International, a consortium popularly known by its former name, International Youth Hostels or its affiliate, American Youth Hostels. Despite the "youth" part, they cater to bargain-seekers of all ages. The annual fee includes a complete directory of North American locations. Contact: Hosteling International, 733 Fifteenth Street NW, Suite 840, Washington, DC 20005; (202) 783-6161.

CAMPING CAPERS

Turtles and snails travel with their dwellings, and so can you. You can save big bucks by combining your transportation and accommodations if you travel and live in the same space. Recreation vehicles, known as RVs, are multi-purpose conveyances offering sleeping, cooking and bathroom facilities on wheels. You can use your own RV or rent one to put a roof over your head at a fraction of the cost of a lodge or condo. An RV can be heated to provide comfortable shelter, and you can spend every night aboard for the duration of your vacation.

Many of America's four hundred or so rental operators are open year-round, including some in or near the snowbelt. Compared with summer rates, winter RV rentals are a steal. Larger motor homes sleep up to six adults, and many feature underfloor storage space for items such as skis and poles, which would clutter up the interior of the unit. Cruise America is the largest nationwide motor home rental operation, with ski-country affiliates in Flagstaff, Sacramento, Denver, Boston, Minneapolis/St. Paul, Billings and Portland, Oregon. Rates vary by location, and many dealers offer free airport pickup to their customers. Reservations (and even fly-drive options) can be made by contacting the company at 5959 Blue Lagoon Drive, Suite 250, Miami, FL 33126; (800) 327-7778. Among the independent agencies to contact are C&T Trailer Supply in Bozeman, Montana (406-587-8610) and Sierra RV Rentals in Reno (702-324-0522).

Rental dealers' way of keeping you honest about heat and such is a hefty deposit, two hundred to five hundred dollars, which is fully refundable when you return the rig unscathed. Normally, you get one hundred free miles a day, and many dealers lower their extra-mileage rate in winter, too. Since neither your automobile insurance nor your credit card's collision damage waiver coverage extends to RVs, you must also count on six to twelve dollars additional per day for insurance. Gas mileage isn't great (seven to ten miles per gallon shouldn't surprise you), but then, a car or van also uses gas, and all the mileage you rack up on skis is the same, no matter where you sleep or how you travel.

A few private campgrounds in the north country remain open in winter. Otherwise, you'll have to plan on self-sufficiency, and some ski areas even invite RVers to park overnight. U.S. Forest Service campgrounds, some of which are near a ski resort, generally are free during the winter. However, there are no hookups, water is normally not available and users are requested to take out their own trash. In either case, instead of conveniences like an electrical outlet, water and waste-disposal systems and perhaps even cable TV, you'll have to operate off the generator and run your propane heater to keep the wastewater holding tanks from freezing (low is okay while you're skiing). In the Rockies, where winters can be brutal, rental agencies do not permit you to fill the water tanks, so you'll have to opt for a wilderness experience of no showers, even if you are camped under a solid roof. Still, you can sleep in a warm place, cook, wash dishes and, with proper antifreeze precautions, use the toilets.

The Recreation Vehicle Industry Association puts out a useful booklet called "Wintertime RV Use and Maintenance." It is two dollars from RVIA, P.O. Box 2999, Reston, VA 22090. For a directory of rental dealers, send $3.50 for the latest "Who's Who in RV Rentals" to the Recreation Vehicle Rental Association, 3251 Old Lee Highway, Suite 500, Fairfax, VA 22030. You can also request a free brochure with general RV, campground, rental and trip-planning information from Go Camping America, P.O. Box 2669, Reston, VA 22090; (800) 47-SUNNY.

PARKING POLICIES

Most ski areas have a no-campers policy, but here are some that welcome skiers and their RVs. Ski areas providing hookups, especially water and sewer, may have a paid rather than a free parking policy:

SKI AREA	CAMPER POLICY
Afton Alps, MN	Reserved camper parking; electrical hookups available
Alpine Meadows, CA	Self-contained campers permitted overnight
Appalachian Ski Mountain, NC	Camper sites with hookups available
Bear Valley, CA	Self-contained campers permitted overnight
Berkshire East, MA	Self-contained campers permitted overnight
The Big Mountain, MT	Self-contained campers permitted overnight
Bolton Valley, VT	Self-contained campers permitted overnight
Brighton, UT	Self-contained campers permitted overnight
Brodie Mountain, MA	150 campsites with hookups available

Burke Mountain, VT	Self-contained campers permitted overnight
Camelback, PA	Self-contained campers permitted overnight
Canaan Valley, WV	Low-cost overnight camper parking permitted
Canyon Ski Area, AB	Overnight parking with electricity available
Catamount Ski Area, NY	Self-contained campers permitted overnight
Cockaigne Ski Area, NY	Camper parking permitted; electrical hookups available
Crystal Mountain, WA	41 camper sites with hookups available
Fortress Mountain, AB	Low-cost campsites with electricity
49 North, WA	Camper parking with hookups available
Frost Ridge Ski Area, NY	150 camper sites (16 winterized) at area
Fun Valley, IA	Camper parking permitted; electrical hookup available
Gore Mountain, NY	Self-contained campers permitted overnight
Gunstock, NH	Self-contained campers permitted overnight
Holiday Valley, NY	Camper sites with electrical hookup
Hoodoo Ski Area, OR	18 camper sites with hookups available
Hunter Mountain, NY	Self-contained campers permitted overnight
Keystone, CO	Self-contained campers permitted overnight
Kimberly Resort, BC	Limited spaces for self-contained campers
King Ridge, NH	Self-contained campers permitted overnight
Lake Louise, AB	Self-contained campers permitted overnight
Mission Ridge, WA	Self-contained campers permitted overnight
Mt. Bachelor, OR	Self-contained (and occupied) campers overnight free at designated parking areas
Mt. Baker, WA	Self-contained campers permitted in designated sites in upper parking lot
Mt. Baldy, CA	Camping area with water hookups

Mt. Snow/Haystack, VT	Self-contained campers permitted overnight
The Pass*, WA	Self-contained campers permitted overnight at designated sites
Pats Peak, NH	Self-contained campers permitted overnight
Peek 'n Peak, NY	Self-contained campers permitted overnight
Potawatomi Park, WI	Camper parking; electrical hookups available
Silver Star, BC	54 RV sites with electrical hookups adjacent to resort
Sipapu, NM	Trailer park with all hookups except water
Ski Apache, NM	Self-contained campers permitted overnight
Ski Liberty, PA	Self-contained campers permitted overnight
Ski Sunrise, CA	Self-contained campers permitted overnight
Ski Windham, NY	Self-contained campers permitted overnight
Snow Ridge, NY	Self-contained campers permitted overnight
Snow Valley, CA	Full hookups available; lower cost without hookups
Sugarbush, VT	Self-contained campers permitted overnight
Sunrise Ski Resort, AZ	Self-contained campers permitted overnight
Taos, NM	Self-contained campers permitted overnight
Timberline, OR	Self-contained campers permitted overnight
Timber Ridge, MI	Self-contained campers permitted overnight
Toggenburg Ski Center, NY	Self-contained campers permitted overnight
Trollhaugen Ski Area, WI	Camper parking permitted; electrical hook-ups available

*Alpental-Snoqualmie-Ski Acres-Hyak

PAID PARKING

RV parks in ski country that are open year-round offer hookups and often such amenities as recreational facilities (pools, saunas, game room, etc.), guest laundry and/or a convenience store. Some are also along a free shuttle bus route to a ski resort. The Lake Tahoe area, Flagstaff near the Arizona Snowbowl and Utah's greater Salt Lake area abound with private campgrounds. Here is a sampling of ski areas with RV parks very close by. Ski-town chambers of commerce and central reservations services can point you to any nearby RV park that is open during the winter:

SKI AREA	RV PARK
Breckenridge, CO	Tiger Run, complete RV resort located along shuttle bus route to all Summit County ski areas
Holiday Valley, NY	Low-cost RV parking across from SnowPine chairlift
Monarch, CO	Good Sam Campground 8 miles east of ski areas
Mt. Bachelor, OR	Bend Kampground Best Holiday Travelpark, Crown Villa RV Park
Mt. Brighton, MI	Campground 4 miles from ski area
Mt. Spokane, WA	Kirk's Lodge, 8 miles from area, has campsites
Park City, UT	Hidden Haven RV Park, 6 miles from town
Steamboat, CO	Ski Time and Fish Creek Campgrounds within 5 miles of ski area
Sun Valley, ID	KOA in Ketchum, 2 miles from lifts
Whistler/Blackcomb, BC	KOA Whistler Campground & RV Park; free shuttle to resort
Whiteface Mountain, NY	KOA 2 miles from area
Wild Mountain Ski Area, MN	Wild River Park, 4 miles from area
Wisp Ski Resort, MD	Campground 2 miles from area

CHAPTER SEVEN

EAT, DRINK AND BE MERRY

S kiers do not live by snowy slopes alone. A successful ski day, weekend or vacation involves eating three squares a day and often after-ski entertainment. Even if you've been cost-cautious with everything else, it's easy to fall off the budgetary wagon when it comes to off-slope expenditures. To spend the very least, rent a condo, food- and booze-shop wisely (if you're driving, you'll save money by going to your hometown supermarket rather than buying groceries at resort prices), have an after-drink in your unit, prepare every meal yourself and eat in and spend your evenings in front of the television. But for many skiers, that's not much of a vacation. You can mix such constraint with free or inexpensive activities and have fun without breaking the bank. Window shopping, art gallery walks and people, watching are free. Many lodging properties have on-site swimming pools, which can provide hours of family fun. Fitness centers, skating rinks and swimming pools are often free or inexpensive for resort guests, and for youngsters, they are a lot cheaper than just a short time of pumping quarters into a video game machine.

STRUCTURE YOUR SKIING FOR VALUE

With smart planning, you can get in a lot of skiing for your money. If you're in line when the lifts open, break early for lunch, ski when others are eating and keep going till the last run, as long as you have the stamina, you can pack more skiing and less waiting into every day. Pack a snack to eat on the lifts (but please dispose of that candy wrapper or apple core properly). If you find long liftlines at popular spots, study the map and try to find alternate routes. This is especially wise, and relatively easy, at large, top-dollar mountains, which usually offer options. If you like fair weather and soft snow, follow the sun and ski east-facing slopes in the morning and west-facing ones in the afternoon. If you're willing to trade a little comfort for shorter liftlines, do the opposite. If you want to ski the corduroy, check the morning grooming report and start on the runs that have been manicured. If you like to ski the bumps, ski the mogul runs early while you're still fresh and the slopes are uncrowded. But don't push your envelope. Patrol statistics indicate that more skiers are injured while taking the proverbial last run than at any time of day. So when you start to poop out, back off and quit until the next day.

START THE DAY WITH A GOOD BREAKFAST . . .

Nutritionists (and moms) always urge active people to fuel up at the beginning of the day. A big breakfast pays dividends in increased energy (i.e., the ability to take more runs without wearing out), and it also can be an economy move. If you're eating out, breakfast is usually the cheapest meal of the day. Carbo-load, but if you're skiing at unaccustomed altitudes, take it easy on grease. A stack of pancakes, a fruit plate with whole-grain bread or a filling granola-type cereal will last longer, feel better and probably cost less than a plate dripping with fried eggs, bacon and potatoes. If you arrive at the ski area early, you can secure a close-in parking space and have a filling breakfast in the cafeteria (you'll probably have instructors and patrollers for company), and you'll be right there to hit the slopes as soon as the lifts open.

. . . OR WITH FIRST TRACKS

In summer, the early bird gets the worm. In winter, the early skier gets a good chunk of a big mountain—and perhaps powder as well. A handful of areas allow a few skiers on the mountain before the lifts, generally, but first-lift, first-tracks policies sometimes require special arrangement. The easiest way to get a head start on the skiing day is simply to show up early. On weekends and holidays, for instance, Stowe cranks up one lift, usually the high-speed quad but sometimes the gondola, at 7:30 A.M., half an hour before the normal opening. Loon Mountain, New Hampshire, opens at 8:00 A.M. on weekends and 8:30 A.M. on weekdays. Regulars at these mountains say that they get in a lot of skiing before the liftlines begin to build around 9:30 A.M., time for early birds to take a coffee break.

Snowbird's day starts at 9:00 A.M. when guests on some packages at the Cliff Lodge have first crack at the First Tram. On a powder morning, this can result in one of skiing's great runs. (Other guests can check with the concierge in advance to see if there's space.) In any case, it doesn't hurt to get in line early, since even the 125 skiers unloading from the First Tram can't carve up the mountain too badly, and there's still a lot of powder

left for the second tram. One morning a week, Sugarloaf's slopes are reserved for early-rising women. Chicks on Sticks, an offshoot of the area's
successful women's programs, invites women to start skiing at 7:30 A.M.
on one midweek morning, an hour and a half before the lifts open. It's
complimentary to women who have a valid lift ticket, but you have to sign
up in advance at the ski school office.

Steamboat charges a few dollars for an earlybird ride on the gondola,
breakfast at the Thunderhead Restaurant and first crack at the powder.
Neighboring Blackcomb and Whistler, British Columbia, have similar programs, with loading on high-speed lifts as early as 7:30 A.M., a buffet
breakfast at their respective mid-mountain restaurants and a shot at the
snow before most skiers have finished their second cups of coffee. Groups
can book Crested Butte's First Tracks Breakfast, including a hearty breakfast at the Paradise Warming House before the mountain opens to the
public.

BROWN BAGGING AND OTHER
MONEY-SAVING TRICKS

Midday meals can take a big chunk out of your skiing budget. Small ski
areas catering to budget-conscious families recognize the problem and often
set aside a special room for brown baggers, which is the nickname for
people who tote their own lunches. Pack a hearty lunch, perhaps augment
it with soup or a hot beverage, and you'll save dollars every day you ski.
If brown bagging isn't officially permitted, you can carry some kind of
lunch in pack or pocket, even munch it on the lift, and go into the lodge
just to rest and have something to drink. Peanut butter sandwiches, something on a bagel, Power Bars or other energy bars and dried fruit hold up
pretty well until you get around to eating them. Dannon, which sponsors
Winterfest, a series of ski-area product samplings and drawings for prizes,
has produced a free skier's nutrition pamphlet that includes cents-off coupons on the company's yogurts. It is available free from Dannon Alpine
Skier's Trail Map Offer, 230 Park Avenue, 11th floor, New York, NY
10003.

If you have to go through the cafeteria line, look for the most filling
choices for the lowest price. Pizza and burritos are favorite choices, and
where they are available, they probably cost less than a burger or sandwich
and an order of fries. A baked-potato bar is another good bet. The spuds
are usually huge, and you can load them up with enough toppings to fuel
you through a hard afternoon of skiing. You usually can't go wrong with
a bowl of soup, especially one laden with rice, beans or noodles. Some ski

areas, like Winter Park, and even Vail, have special-value lunches for thrifty skiers available every day. Blackcomb, British Columbia, has a special children's counter in the new Glacier Creek on-mountain lodge with well-priced, suitably portioned children's lunches.

DINE LIKE A LOCAL

Cooking your own meals is an obvious way to cut down on expenses, but you can also eat economically if you do as the residents do. Don't just read the chamber of commerce visitors guide, but also scan the resort town's newspaper. These papers are often free (or they sometimes cost just a quarter). You'll find coupons to clip for two-for-one dinner offers and ads for other meal sales, happy-hour specials, all-you-can-eat salad bars or buffets, early-bird pricing, children's specials and other money-saving offers. Brochure racks in hotel and condo lobbies, convenience stores and ski shops contain a wealth of information and discount coupons for all sorts of goods and services.

END THE DAY WITH A FREE PARTY

Full ski weeks, special programs like women's workshops and racing clinics, college ski weeks and ski-club trips generally include some après-ski events. They may be wine-and-cheese welcome socials, mountain barbecue, informational sessions on nutrition, ski conditioning and the like and an awards ceremony or closing party. At some resorts, entertainment at least one afternoon a week is available free to anyone who shows up. The Big Mountain, Montana, ski school hosts a Powder Hour every Monday, not just for people in classes but for all guests. It takes place at a popular bar called Moguls and includes complimentary beer, snacks and entertainment. Every Sunday and Thursday, the Whistler Conference Center in British Columbia's largest resort is open for an evening social, providing guests the opportunity to meet instructors, enjoy complimentary refreshments and enter a drawing for prizes. Ski Windham, New York, puts on TGIF Ski Days every Friday from January through March with a fun race and an après-ski party in the Legends Lounge. Burke Mountain, Vermont, kicks off weekends with Friday Fun, featuring big-screen TV with regional sports programming, beverage specials and a tavern menu for adults and table tennis, pool and a jukebox for the younger set. The idea is to welcome weekend skiers with inexpensive entertainment—and to send ski-weekers off with congeniality. A variety of family-oriented activities after the lifts close is also a big drawing card at Smugglers' Notch, Vermont. At Beaver Creek, Colorado, families flock to Thursday Night Lights, a twilight ski down the Haymeadow run accompanied by music and fireworks. Vail joins Beaver Creek in putting on Hot Winter Nights, a free show performed on select Wednesday evenings during the ski season. It features a choreographed run by the renowned ski school's demonstration team, fireworks, music and other entertainment.

Other traditions are more irreverent. The Big Mountain's Frabert starts at 5:30 P.M. every Wednesday at the Bierstube, when the ski patrol good-naturedly awards Clod of the Week honors and taps a keg of free beer. Massanutten, Virginia, celebrates Elvis's birthday the first weekend in January. Monday Night Football at Copper Mountain's B-Lift Pub features big-screen TV and drink specials, and one of Jay Peak's popular parties is the annual Super Bowl bash. Killington does an entire Super Bowl Weekend, with lift/lodging/entertainment packages. The events kick off on Friday night and finish when the game is over. Highlights include a cheerleading contest and a tailgate party. Sunday River has a two-day Super Bowl party with lift and lodging specials, plus a party with zany halftime antics. When you are planning your trip, or even after you arrive at your destination, be sure to check out other local after-ski customs and plug into a low-cost or no-cost party.

Seek out resorts offering special entertainment for the holidays for hours of free or inexpensive diversion. Belleayre, New York, kicks winter off with an annual Homecoming Weekend (Thanksgiving), with a parade, picture taking, free snowflake ornaments for children and a DJ playing Top Ten hits from every year since the area's opening in 1949. Any skier with a valid Thanksgiving Day lift ticket is invited to a complimentary turkey dinner at Sunday River's South Ridge Base Lodge. One of the many well-priced packages offered by San Valley, Idaho, is the Thanksgiving Package, including a lavish holiday buffet. The chefs at Winter Park, Colorado, prepare an elegant Thanksgiving dinner at the mountaintop Lodge at Sunspot. It may not be cheap, but it is wonderful.

WINTER FESTIVALS FOR FREE FUN

Many ski towns also produce elaborate winter carnivals to stir up interest during midwinter's slack period, which normally means January in the U.S. and February in Canada. The granddaddy of major fests is Steamboat Springs' Winter Carnival, started back in 1913 for local ranch families and cowhands. It maintains its distinctive western atmosphere, and visitors and locals alike love the five days of nonstop activities, many of them free. Ski racing, freestyle and jumping exhibitions and a downtown parade featuring Steamboat Spring's high school band, which skis instead of marches, and a fantastic evening show highlight the week.

The Stowe Winter Carnival, Vermont's classic, features a village block party, an inexpensive chicken pot pie supper open to all, ski events, snow-golf and snow-volleyball, dogsled and snowshoe events, a masked ball with a bargain admission fee and a cheap Karnival Karaoke evening. The Quebec Winter Carnival in Quebec City is the Canadian version of Mardi Gras. Grandiose snow sculptures, parades, races across the frozen St. Lawrence River and enough liquid lightning to thaw out the most bone-chilled soul are highlights of this fantastic and frenzied citywide party. Red River puts on the New Mexican version of Mardi Gras, complete daily parades, costume parties, nightly family-style balls, torchlight parades and even Cajun cookin'. Aspen's Winterskol is a huge January event that brightens the post-New Year's doldrums. Other ski towns with notable winter carnivals include Banff, Alberta; Durango, Colorado; Hanover, New Hampshire (Dartmouth Winter Carnival, easy access from many New England ski resorts); Jackson, New Hampshire; Laconia/Gunstock, New Hampshire; McCall, Idaho; North Lake Tahoe/Truckee, California; Red River, New Mexico; Saranac Lake, New York; Schweitzer/Sandpoint, Idaho; Sun Valley, Idaho; Telluride, Colorado; Whitefish, Montana; and Winter Park/Fraser Valley, Colorado.

Carnivals and special events are also invading December and even late November calendars. The Northern Lights celebration is one of the highlights of the Lake Tahoe North Shore. A Christmas gala, torchlight parade, the Festival of Trees & Lights, Brunch With Santa and the World's Largest Office Party are highlights of this early December extravaganza, but for skiers, one of the best reasons to attend is four days of free skiing at Diamond Peak, Nevada. Breckenridge, Colorado, is another special events champ. The town swings into the season in late November (concurrent hot-air balloon festival, street party and microbrew tastings), follows quickly with the Lighting of Breckenridge the first Saturday in December (an evening parade with Santa, a flatbed full of carolers, and spectators joining the procession down Main Street till the Christmas tree is lit), and after the first of the year segues into January. That's when the town puts on an international snow sculpture contest and Ullr Fest, a lighthearted tribute to the Norse god of snow and winter. The former gives visitors good reason to wander the streets and watch the talented artists, while the latter features a parade, nightly parties, "Ullympic" competitions and even a grand ball.

Mammoth Mountain's spectacular Night of Lights, which starts with a flag parade in the late afternoon and culminates with bonfires, caroling and fabulous fireworks, takes place the week before Christmas. In late November, Santa Claus stops at Schweitzer Mountain, Idaho, where he presides over the village light-up. Free or low-cost holiday activities include cooking and crafts classes, a gift fair in the day lodge, Teddy's Berry, Beary Christmas Party for children and a Christmas Eve torchlight parade. Santa is even busier on Christmas itself, for he pays visits, on skis or off, to many ski slopes across the country.

In addition to the many areas that feature special events on Christmas Eve, torchlight parades, where ski pros snake down the mountain carrying flaming torches, are ski-country New Year's Eve traditions that make what we think of as one of the most expensive nights of the year one of the cheapest. Watch the parade, have an early dinner, catch the fireworks and turn on the tube to watch midnight in New York, and be ready to ski on New Year's Day, when the slopes are normally not crowded. South Lake Tahoe and Whistler Village are among the resorts where First Night rings in the new year with alcohol-free festivities, which is a great idea when you realize that New Year's Day (along with Super Bowl Sunday) presents an annual opportunity for great skiing with no liftlines and virtually empty slopes. Steamboat showcases torchlight parades on New Year's Eve, in late January, on Valentine's Day and on St. Patrick's Day.

It's party time when a major ski race comes around. The big meets are the World Cups, and the most action-filled of those are the Alpine events at which such top ski-racing names as Tommy Moe, Picabo Street, AJ Kitt and Alberto Tomba compete. When you watch them, you watch the best. These races have been held in such major North American resorts as Vail, Aspen, Steamboat, Park City, Breckenridge, Lake Louise and Mont Ste.-Anne. Freestyle, disabled and Nordic competitions also provide great opportunities to see top athletes in lower-profile events compete. There is also an active professional ski-racing circuit. Unlike the Alpine World Cup, where skiers race against the clock, one at a time, the pros race on tight parallel courses in elimination heats. They are thrilling to watch, and they often lead to some great après-ski racing action. National, regional and Junior Olympic meets have built-in excitement, too.

Some festivals have a commercial tie rather than a community or competitive origin. You can hook onto the traveling shows that promoters of various products mount at ski areas around the country and across the winter calendar. Dannon Winterfest includes free product sampling and entertainment. A DJ presides over the free festivities, which take place in a tent, including a dance contest and a trivia contest. Even the sampling isn't trivial—have you priced a yogurt in a ski-lodge cafeteria lately? The

Snickers Ski Festival features nine days of family-oriented events—and enough samples of the popular candy bar to rival a Halloween haul. Molson Rocks the Mountain, Jose Cuervo Games of Winter and other promotions sponsored by beer and liquor companies are fun, free and available to those of legal drinking age.

Late March in the East and Midwest and April in the West are a time for fun races, silly costumes, live music on the mountain and all manners of smile-provoking entertainment. Bolton Valley's Spring Fever, Copper Mountain's Spring Fling and Eenie Weenie Bikini Contest, Crested Butte's Flauschink, Jay Peak's Beach Party, Telluride's Surf the Rockies and Winter Park's Spring Closing Day are some of the festivities you should try.

CHAPTER EIGHT

HIDDEN TREASURES

Big may be beautiful, but small is smart. The rock-bottom price for a straightforward high-speed quad chairlift is $2 million, and snow groomers start at $120,000 per machine. When you select a major area that has invested heavily in such equipment, as well as additional millions for large-scale snowmaking and elaborate lodges at the base and perhaps the summit, those costs are reflected in the price of a lift ticket—and often every other service or item of merchandise an area sells or rents. Still, big ski resorts do excite us. We love to ski the mountains, explore the towns, drop the names. We wish we had more money, more time, better skiing ability, better clothes. Big resorts make us feel important for being there, insignificant because no one knows we're there. We are thrilled at the scale, frustrated because a week is never long enough to get into the groove.

By contrast, small areas please us financially and in other ways, too. We feel important because by the third round, lift operators greet us like old friends, or at least longtime acquaintances. We are secure because our kids can't get lost—heck, we adults don't get lost—and we usually don't feel compelled to separate or lock our skis. And darned if the skiing isn't good, the lines aren't short and the experience isn't as comfortable as an old leather boot. Yet in skiing, "small" is a very fluid word that can carry several definitions. Often, a small ski area is just plain small, best described as a ski hill with a modest vertical and few facilities. Other times, it is one with rather expansive terrain but a modest infrastructure. Sometimes, a ski area is "small" only in contrast with a nearby giant.

Consider the context of an alluring ski mountain with a big name, huge scale and a complex infrastructure and a small, low-cost one, and remember that you can only make a turn at a time. That turn can be just as satisfying whether you have 1,500 vertical feet of mountain above and below you or just 150 feet. Even some of the country's best racers have grown up on small, simple ski hills. Olympic bronze medalist Cindy Nelson started skiing at Lutsen, Minnesota (600 vertical feet); former pro-racing champ and TV commentator Hank Kashiwa made his early turns on McCauley Mountain, New York (633 feet); and AJ Kitt, one of the most exciting downhill racers of the 1990s, spent his early years at Swain Mountain, New York (650 feet). Such small ski areas are sometimes ends unto themselves, especially if you have one near your home. But modest areas can even find a place in your vacation plans. Perhaps you can't envision a whole week at Mt. Mellow, but when you are vacationing at a mega-mountain, a day or two spent at a mini is worth considering for your budget and your spirit.

SKI CLOSE TO HOME

Some of the best values are found at modestly sized areas very close to metropolitan areas. They often do such volume business that they can keep rates low. Not only is the skiing cheaper than at bigger, more distant mountains, but you'll also have lower travel expenses and less travel time. Many such areas offer night skiing at a considerable savings, too. Four Lakes Village and Villa Olivia are just north of Chicago. Boston Mills and Brandywine are fifteen miles from Cleveland. Five small ski hills are located in an arc within half-an-hour's drive from metropolitan Detroit. Nearly a dozen circle Minneapolis-St. Paul. Within fifty miles of New York City and its northern New Jersey suburbs, Hidden Valley, Craigmeur and Campgaw all offer modestly priced skiing. Pennsylvania's Poconos ski areas lie within two hours of Philadelphia and New York. Blue Hills is ten miles south of Boston, Mt. Southington is seventeen miles southwest of Hartford, Bogus Basin is sixteen miles from Boise and Sandia Peak is half-an-hour from Albuquerque. Eldora, which is half-an-hour from Boulder and about an hour from Denver, is such a budget-oriented ski area that it actually lowered its lift ticket from thirty-two dollars to thirty dollars the same year that Aspen raised its top price from fifty dollars to fifty-two dollars.

If you live in one of a very few charmed cities, you can enjoy nearby skiing on mountains of considerable size. Loveland, a little more than an hour west of Denver, has an economical ticket and one of the most competitive frequent-skier programs in Colorado. Alta, Brighton, Snowbasin, Solitude and Wolf Mountain, all within an hour of Salt Lake City, are less expensive than Deer Valley, Park City or Snowbird. The tiny Cochran Ski Area near Burlington, Vermont, has really low-priced tickets, but the larger resorts of Bolton Valley and Smugglers' Notch still charge significantly less than giant Sugarbush or Stowe. Anchorage skiers view giant Alyeska as the largest and most expensive of the three local areas, but it's big enough to rank as a major destination for skiers from as far away as Tokyo.

You really do have to comparison shop, however, since small, close-in areas may not necessarily save you really big bucks over more distant, larger ones, although you can still pare travel time. If you live in Los Angeles, you might appreciate saving freeway mileage by skiing Mt. Baldy or even Bear Mountain and Snow Summit near Big Bear Lake, which are within day-trip range, over Mammoth Mountain, which is far enough to require a weekend. Little Wachusett Mountain and tiny Nashoba Valley are just over an hour from Boston, less than half the drive of even New Hampshire's closest areas, and they charge just a few dollars less than their northern neighbors.

SKI FAR FROM HOME

If you are willing to invest road time to reap the dividends of saved dollars, you can follow a contrarian strategy and go to the farthest reach of what is a reasonable day or weekend trip from a major metropolitan area. For instance, Balsams/Wilderness, New Hampshire's northernmost ski area, charges a third less for weekend skiing than the state's most expensive ski resorts—and far less for midweek skiing. Burke Mountain in Vermont's scenic Northeast Kingdom comes in with the lowest prices of any good-sized area in the state. Similarly, several of Colorado's best snow and lowest prices are found at several ski areas more than the customary two-hour day-trip distance from Denver or Colorado Springs. Therefore, you'll find great rates (and no parking fees) at Monarch, Ski Cooper and Wolf Creek. All three are midsized mountains with simple lift systems. Another reason that they are able to keep prices low is that they are at such high elevations that they don't need snowmaking. Similarly, Powder Mountain and Snow-basin, which are slightly more than fifty miles from Salt Lake City, have lower-priced lift tickets than most of the areas within thirty miles.

SELECT A SMALL AREA

Large glamorous resorts not only charge more than small, no-frills ones for lifts, but everything from parking fees to potato chips is likely to be higher as well. If you have your heart set on a particular mountain range, you can often enjoy similar climate, snow conditions and scenery at a smaller neighbor. If you are vacationing, you may need to commute a bit between your lodgings and the lifts, but that's an easy trade-off for kindness to your budget.

In central Vermont, Suicide Six is a challenging little hill with rock-bottom midweek prices and weekend rates that are far less than nearby Killington or Okemo. Up north, Bolton Valley and Jay Peak charge less than Stowe or Sugarbush. Of the New Hampshire areas that promote themselves as the Ski 93 group, Bretton Woods charges less than Loon Mountain or Waterville Valley, and over the Mt. Washington Valley, moderately sized Black Mountain and smaller King Pine are less expensive than Attitash, Cranmore or Wildcat (especially on weekends). Sometimes small areas compete against each other. Ragged Mountain, located in south-central New Hampshire very close to four other modest mountains, held its adult lift-ticket prices to twenty-five dollars on weekends and twelve dollars on weekdays for five consecutive seasons to keep its competitive edge.

The same story holds true in the West. Salt Lake City skiers enjoy nearby ski areas that come in a variety of styles and prices. The contrasts in Utah are the most dramatic, with Alta, Brighton, Solitude and Wolf Mountain priced less than Deer Valley, Park City or Snowbird. In the Lake Tahoe area, you can ski in closer harmony with your budget at Boreal Ridge, Diamond Peak, Homewood, Soda Springs, Tahoe Donner and especially Donner Ski Ranch and tiny Granlibakken, than at such giants as Alpine Meadows, Heavenly Ski Resort and Squaw Valley. Of the three ski areas operating on the flanks of Oregon's Mt. Hood, Mt. Hood Meadows is the largest, with lift tickets significantly higher than its smaller neighbors, Mt. Hood Snowbowl and Timberline. Alyeska, Alaska's giant, is about an hour's drive from Anchorage. Hilltop Ski Area and Alpenglow at Arctic Valley are half the driving time and a fraction of the cost.

Elsewhere, you won't find such a dense concentration of areas. Colorado's Ski Sunlight, a midsized mountain roughly equidistant between Aspen and Vail, sells lift tickets that are far less than either of its larger neighbors. SilverCreek, between Steamboat and Winter Park, specializes in beginners and bargains. Lookout Pass, at the Idaho/Montana state line, is only open Thursdays through Sundays but charges about 40 percent less than Silver Mountain. In northern New Mexico, a lift ticket at Taos costs a few dollars more than smaller Angel Fire, Red River, Pajarito or Ski Rio. Arizona Snowbowl is the state's largest ski area, and the Williams Ski Area is the smallest, yet both are easily accessible from Flagstaff, but Snowbowl's weekend lift ticket price is one-third more than Williams's, and on weekdays, the big area charges twice what the little one does.

Occasionally, a small ski area operating almost under the nose of a bigger one makes a nice change of pace during a ski vacation. You can use it for a warm-up day, a cool-down day, night skiing, or as an opportunity to ski with the locals. Howelsen Ski Area, still known by locals as Howelsen Hill, is the steep little area where Steamboat Springs' homegrown ski-jumping and freestyle champions have trained. Its modest 440-foot vertical and thirteen runs could be tucked virtually unnoticed into nearby Steamboat's far-reaching terrain, but its rates are a real eye-opener. In 1995-96, the area sold a child's *season pass* for ten dollars. With night skiing, ice skating at the base, the opportunity to watch some of America's best skiers and a location just a block from Steamboat's main street, a visit to Howelsen dovetails neatly into a Steamboat vacation. The biggest little hill, Snow King on the outskirts of Jackson, Wyoming, is the friendly neighbor of one of the nation's biggest of the big areas, Jackson Hole. These two, plus Grand Targhee, now co-operate on an interchangeable multiday ticket to encourage vacationers to ski around and sample areas of all sizes. Other similar situations are The Little Ski Hill in McCall, Idaho, near Brundage Mountain and Hesperus, west of Durango. Far bigger and far more famous Purgatory is north of town.

Occasionally, even neighboring ski areas owned by the same corporations have different ticket prices. Colorado's Arapahoe Basin has a lower-priced lift ticket (plus better snow and a longer season) than Keystone or Breckenridge. Arrowhead will eventually be linked into Beaver Creek, but until it is, prices are less than at The Beave or nearby Vail. Vermont's Haystack is cheaper than Mt. Snow, just up the road.

K.I.S.S. (OR, KEEP IT SIMPLE, SKIER)

Of all the ski-area statistics for skiers to calculate, vertical and lift capacity are two of the most important. Vertical is the difference between the base and summit elevations. A rule of thumb (except in the Midwest where a 600-foot vertical is a giant) is that a small ski area is one with less than a 1,000-foot vertical, a midsized area has between 1,000 and 2,000 and a large area has more than 2,000. Lift capacity is the number of skiers per hour who can be transported uphill if every seat on every chair is filled. With the exception of Alta (9,100), Bogus Basin (6,700), Powder Mountain (6,350), Red Lodge (6,400), Snowbasin (7,400) and Wolf Mountain (6,700), none of the K.I.S.S. areas below have a capacity exceeding 5,000 skiers per hour—although they do fall into the category of medium or large areas in terms of vertical. As a comparison, Vail's capacity approaches 45,000 skiers per hour.

When skiers are surveyed on the best bargain in U.S. skiing, Alta, Utah, heads the list. This classic ski area at the head of Little Cottonwood Canyon has a respectable 2,000-foot vertical, a reputation for a gut-wrenching challenge, an average annual snowfall of five hundred inches and a daily lift ticket that's routinely several dollars less than Snowbird, a mile away in the same canyon. Alta keeps rates down because snowmaking is not necessary and the lifts include two triple and six double chairlifts, some of them of classic vintage. Elsewhere in Utah, which has to be considered America's budget skiing capital, Beaver Mountain, Elk Meadows, Nordic Valley, Powder Mountain, Snowbasin and Wolf Mountain offer substantial terrain and lodges with moderate prices, but no fancy lifts. You'll find a similar philosophy at other mountains too. Colorado's Cuchara, Monarch, Powderhorn, Ski Cooper, Ski Sunlight and Wolf Creek don't have a high-speed quad among them, but their lift tickets are ten dollars to twenty dollars (or more) lower than the state's giants.

Montana has a reputation as being rugged. So many of its appropriately rugged ski areas have prices that have the stamp of yesteryear that it's the uncrowned king of K.I.S.S. Montana Snowbowl, with its humongous and astonishingly challenging 2,600-foot vertical but just two chairlifts, one T-bar and a simple A-frame base lodge, is the classic K.I.S.S. area. Close behind are Bridger Bowl with a 2,000-foot lift-served vertical and an additional 500 feet of hike-up terrain for experts; Red Lodge with 2,016 feet; Marshall Ski Area with 1,500 feet; Discovery Basin and Great Divide, each with verticals of about 1,300 feet. You might think that the ultimate bargain is Maverick Mountain, a weekend area with 2,020 vertical feet, one chairlift, one ski tow and an all-day adult lift ticket price that at this writing still hadn't cracked twenty dollars. But no, Turner Mountain in Montana's northwest corner does it even better, with 2,165 vertical feet of mostly advanced terrain, one T-bar and a lift ticket that may have risen to fifteen dollars by the time you read this. Idaho is America's runner-up K.I.S.S.-er. Pebble Creek with 2,000 feet of vertical, Bogus Basin with 1,800, Brundage Mountain with 1,500 and Soldier Mountain with 1,400 feet are all sizable areas with very inexpensive tickets. If you ski any of these obscure areas, you'll find comparably cheap accommodations but perhaps a half-hour or so away.

Vermont's Mad River Glen is the Alta of the East. This barebones classic, surrounded by the glitter of Sugarbush and Sugarbush North, remains true to its frugal Yankee roots. Just four chairlifts, including the last remaining single chair in the Northeast, serve 2,000 vertical feet of largely challenging skiing. Snowmaking and other frills are minimal, and lift prices match. At this writing, a group of loyal Mad River skiers had just bought the area from its longtime owner. Their intention is to retain the low-key, low-cost atmosphere, and they are willing to invest to do so.

The other contender in Vermont's lots-for-little stakes is Burke Mountain, which also has 2,000 vertical feet but a few more lifts, and Saddleback is the Maine version, with two chairlifts and three T-bars serving a 1,830-foot vertical. The area prices its midweek, nonholiday lift tickets at incredibly low prices. In 1994-95, for instance, the fifteen dollar early-season lift ticket and two-for-one lodging essentially from Thanksgiving to Christmas was beaten only when the tickets dropped to five dollars a day the first week in December or when Ski Maine Learn to Ski Free Week was celebrated for free intros the following week. In late January, the price again fell to ten dollars. Prices and policies may vary in future seasons, but you can bet that they'll be hard to beat.

CHAPTER NINE

THE GROUP

S kiing may be an individual sport, but it is also an extremely social
activity. People like to ski with friends, family members or even
with new acquaintances whom they've met at the slopes. When
enough people get together, the economies of scale kick in. You
can reap these savings by joining a group, or if you can't find one that
suits your tastes, needs or location, start your own.

JOIN A CLUB

The ski club has been a fixture of the American skiing scene practically as
long as the sport itself. In fact, the first was the Ishpeming Ski Club,
founded on Michigan's Upper Peninsula in 1887. It promoted ski jumping, kicked off the National Ski Fall of Fame and is still thriving. During
the first ski wave of this century, other clubs were formed to purchase
houses in the mountains so that their city-dwelling members would have
a congenial home away from home and a built-in system of buddies with
whom to ski and travel. The Schussverein Ski Club was established in
1932 by a group of Harvard graduates just for that purpose. Clubs were
also founded by alumni of other prestigious universities to foster sports-
manlike ski racing or to enable well-born skiers to mingle on the slopes
with their own.

Clubs mushroomed along with the pre- and post-World War II skiing
boom. Every skier either belonged to a club or knew someone who did.
To understand how important ski clubs were to the growth of skiing,
remember that this was before the Interstate highway system, toll-free
central reservations services or slopeside condominium developments. It
was, however, a time of energy and enthusiasm, and young skiers flocked
to fledgling ski areas to make some turns, perhaps race and probably party.
The ski club was the perfect framework during the sport's infancy. The
high profile that clubs once enjoyed has faded, but the popularity of clubs

has not. Their numbers are stronger than ever.

Clubs still provide a companionable and economical way to ski. Dues are modest, generally between twenty dollars and fifty dollars a year, for which members receive such benefits as an annual ski swap, bus trips to nearby ski areas and extremely well-priced ski vacations (and sometimes summer adventure trips) to distant or exotic resorts. They also are excellent social organizations, providing such hometown activities as meetings combined with a social hour, picnics, local hikes, get-in-shape-to-ski sessions, slide shows and community-service opportunities. Some clubs are heavily geared to singles, others are populated by families, still others attract older skiers and some are large enough to contain various demographic subgroups. And yes, a few still maintain their own old-style ski houses. But clubs' focus has changed from close-by skiing to economical travel. Many groups are large enough to carry a lot of clout with airlines, motor coach operators and ski resorts, and they can negotiate excellent group rates on various components of a ski trip. Since much of the labor involved in organizing trips is done by volunteers, clubs don't mark up packages or take commissions, which translates into savings that are passed on to members. (Officers and trip leaders are compensated by free travel, which is the ultimate reward for all that hard work.)

Ski-club trips are easy on the budget and the schedule, since they are organized from the nearest gateway city and include the basics such as transportation, lift tickets and lodging. They also include built-in activities, including races, mountain picnics, welcome parties, awards parties, sometimes sight-seeing options and perhaps other extras. Ski areas love clubs and often reward them (and by extension, loyal members) with further benefits. Groups booking trips to Stratton, Vermont, may qualify for additional days there or at nearby Okemo, or in Canada at Tremblant, Quebec; Panorama, British Columbia; or Blackcomb, British Columbia. At other areas, elaborate "club appreciation days" feature especially inexpensive lift tickets, races and other fun events, and perhaps a free barbecue on the mountain or an after-ski party. Saddleback, Maine, hosts a New Year's potluck for ski-club families—a suitably low-key event for this casual ski area.

The staple of ski clubs is a group bus trip. If you live within day or weekend range of sizable ski destinations but would rather not drive, say, from Baltimore, Washington or Philadelphia to New England or from Kansas City to Colorado, a club bus trip may make the difference between skiing and staying home. The fact that clubs usually get about a 25 percent price break when they deliver a busload of skiers to an area just adds to the attraction of not driving. Some clubs, especially those in the Midwest, have their own sleeper buses outfitted with bunks for weekend ski trips with overnight travel to the Colorado Rockies. Other clubs own or lease houses, with various arrangements for use. Most houses are available on a first-come, first-served (or first-reserved, first-served) basis. Others, like the San Francisco Ski Club, offer shares, with other members welcome when space is available.

The country's nearly 3,500 individual clubs provide benefits to an estimated 1.25 million members. Because of the travel deals that large groups can swing, the country's biggest ski clubs tend to be far from snow-covered mountains. Kansas City, St. Louis, Dallas and even Miami have huge clubs. Clubs are clustered in some forty-five "councils," which also organize trips and offer further benefits. Most of the councils are regional, and some, like the huge Texas Ski Council and Florida Ski Council, put together legendary ski trips to great resorts at unbeatable prices. In addition to individual clubs' offerings, for instance, the Texas council generally organizes five major ski trips each winter, the Florida council arranges three and the Chicago council two.

Other associations reflect the common interests of constituent clubs. Some are linked by an interest in recreational racing (Rokka League), age (Over The Hill Gang), disability (National Handicapped Sports Federation), ethnicity (National Brotherhood of Skiers for black skiers or Asian Skiers International) or profession (North American Airline Ski Federation). Ski Utah, a trade association of ski areas in the state, formed a club aimed at newcomers to the Salt Lake City area who are accustomed to traditional ski-club benefits, incentives and socializing opportunities. Major employers and large plants sometimes have their own ski clubs. United Airlines nationally, Merck in Pennsylvania, General Electric in upstate New York and the Pentagon in the Washington, DC, area are among those with ski clubs.

Such clubs often band together in local recreational racing leagues, with a season-long calendar of competitions and well-priced merriment at hills with night skiing. Utah's Winter Sports Park, which is the designated ski-jumping site for the 2002 Winter Olympics, even hosts a bowling-league-style series for amateur ski jumpers. In addition, members of any club may participate in interclub vacation packages. America's Ski Club Week, an annual ski vacation sponsored by *The National Ski Club Newsletter*, is practically cheaper than staying home. The 1995 version to Steamboat, Colorado, costs as little as $399 per person (based on six people sharing a two-bedroom condominium) or $496 (four people in a two-bedroom condo) for six nights of lodging, five days of skiing, daily after-ski parties and various optional extras. Discount airfares were also offered. Other annual trips open to all ski club members include the U.S. Recreational Ski Association's (see page 124) Nation's Ski Week and World Ski Party and National Ski Club Week, held at Sun Valley, Idaho (800-322-2166). Whistler Resort, British Columbia, schedules its annual Ski Club Week for five midweek days before Christmas.

ORGANIZE A GROUP AND SKI FREE
START A FORMAL SKI CLUB . . .

If you know skiers and can devote the time to organizing them into a group, you'll get free skiing, a network of like-minded friends and occasional organizational hassles. Getting deals on skiing and trips is easier than you might think. SkiGroup is a series of trade shows held each spring in about thirty cities across the country where ski resorts and tour operators market their most attractive deals to ski-club officers (see "How to Organize a Trip," on page 123).

. . . OR AN INFORMAL ONE

If you can just get twenty or more people together for a day, weekend or even week of skiing now and then, contact the group sales manager at the ski resort of your choice. You probably can negotiate a favorable group rate and perhaps get some entertainment extras thrown in as the group size increases, especially if you are planning to ski at any but the busiest weekends and holidays. Think about people who ski. Some extended families, co-workers, classmates, religious or fraternal organizations or people who once shared a ski house get together to ski or hold annual or periodic reunions at ski resorts. In summer, groups like this might organize a picnic. In winter, it can be a ski trip.

BE A VOLUNTEER TRIP LEADER

School groups, church groups, scout troops and other youth organizations often organize ski trips. Belleayre, New York, has been promoting low-cost Scout Days for ten years. They take place in early March and offer bargain lift lower-mountain tickets for scout troops, including scouts' families. They also throw in rental equipment discounts and cafeteria specials. Scouts have the opportunity to work toward ski merit badges. Such programs can probably be set up with other areas too. Outdoor-education classes often run trips—for credit and not—to Colorado's Snow Mountain Ranch, which specializes in school and other youth groups. If you volunteer

to chaperone, you'll be joining a lively group on a budget ski vacation—
and often, you'll go along for free.

HOW TO ORGANIZE A TRIP

Whether you start a real club or an ad hoc one to get good deals for yourself
and your friends, as trip leader, you'll have lots of help in setting up a trip.
The typical deal for a club day-trip is group-rate lifts, with one ticket free
for every twenty, or sometimes twenty-five, purchased. Since most motor
coaches hold forty-two people, you can get two free tickets if you fill the
bus. Ski-vacation packages generally include transportation, discounted
lodging and lift tickets, social events and/or races for the group and optional
rental equipment, instruction and other extras at attractive rates. Again,
the norm is one free for every twenty paid vacations. Occasionally, a better
ratio of free-per-paid is offered or can be negotiated.

Ski areas also invite officers and trip chairs to visit. Such "fam trips,"
which are real bargains, are the bonus officers receive for the work they
put into the club. If you are launching a club, you can attend the nearest
SkiGroup show (800-466-1411). Travel providers try to sell their destination to people like you, and you might be invited on a fam or two. Sugarbush, Vermont, has offered an additional trip incentive to organizers who
bring twenty or more people to the resort. When the group stays four
nights or longer on a Ski & Stay package, the leader gets a certificate for
a free pair of Nordica boots or Kästle skis.

But don't be seduced by added incentives if the trip isn't right for your
group. Before you call the resort's group sales office, nail down the dates
you wish to travel and have a good handle on the size of the group and
the budget. The salespeople can help you put together the most attractive
package. Make a list of everything you or a member of your group might
want to know, and don't be shy about asking detailed questions, such as
the location of accommodations, housekeeping policies, maximum occupancy per unit, shuttle buses and others so that you have answers to the
questions your group might in turn ask you. Once the trip is solidified,
hold a meeting, collect deposits and be prepared to respond to questions
and crises as they arise.

Most tour operators can arrange group trips, but a few actually specialize. Moguls Ski & Sun Tours (800-666-4857) offers a series called Feature
Tours, organized for certain destinations in the Rockies during specific
dates. The tour operator then provides detailed instructions and collateral
material to help trip leaders organize and promote a well-priced ski vacation. As further incentive, the company invites one person to travel free

for every fifteen paid participants in a Feature Tour. Gray Rocks, Quebec, discounts all group packages by 10 percent and gives one complimentary stay for every sixteen adults in a group. If you are unable to rally that many people, but can organize eight adventurous skiers looking for a winter trip to the northern Rockies, Off The Beaten Path (800-445-2995) is a tour operator that gives one cross-country skiing trip with the purchase of eight. You can take the free trip as a reward for doing the organizing or split the savings among the participants.

Some individual properties are especially well suited for groups. If your groups wants to go funky, consider Colorado's Snow Mountain Ranch/ YMCA of the Rockies (970-887-2152) with varied accommodations from dorms to cabins, easy access to Winter Park and SilverCreek, sixty-five kilometers of on-site cross-country trails, ski rental, indoor pool, gym and roller skating make this spread one of the country's best for groups of young skiers. If sleek is your style, the SnowCap Lodge at Sunday River, Maine, or Mountain Lair at Crested Butte, Colorado, are modern hotels designed for groups, with a four-per-room setup, ample bathrooms and on-site diversions such as pools, game rooms or snack bars. Smugglers' Notch, Vermont, has developed a package called the Ultimate High School Getaway to attract group organizers. Tour operators specializing in setting up youth and student groups include Ski Masters (209-466-0820) and Los Angeles Ski and Sun Tours (310-546-9641) on the West Coast, Tours de Sport (310-546-9641) and Moguls Ski and Sun Tours (800-666-4857), which is based in Colorado but organizes programs all over the country.

JOIN THE BIG KAHUNA OF SKI CLUBS

The U.S. Recreational Ski Association provides many of the benefits of a ski card, but beyond that, it operates like a supersized ski club. Founded in 1930, this not-for-profit association is the nation's only consumer organization promoting and lobbying for skiing while now offering three levels of dues and member benefits. All members receive USRSA's National Lift Ticket, which functions like a commercial ski card. It offers one free day of skiing at one of about forty-five participating resorts and additional half-price and other discounted lift tickets through the season. Additional budget benefits include values on lodging, ski instruction, equipment rentals and purchases, travel and dining. Membership includes ski-theft insurance and subscriptions to skiing magazines. USRSA also offers deeply discounted vacations and Club 195, which provides space-available three-night, three-day nonholiday getaway ski packages at participating ski areas. As a California-based organization, its benefits are skewed to West Coast ski areas. For membership information, contact United States Recreational Ski Association, P.O. Box 25469, Anaheim, CA 92825-5469; (714) 634-1050.

PARTICIPATE IN AD HOC CLUBS

To attract people to the slopes during quiet midweek periods, many ski areas put together special-interest skiing days. "Ladies' Days," designed for housewives, entered the skiing scene in the 1950s. "Men's Days" soon followed. Now numerous areas also host special programs for seniors as well. Because they attract regular participants, they often take on a special clubbiness and camaraderie, as well as being excellent values. Women's seminars, adult racing clinics and other special-interest programs are attractive offshoots of these old-line programs. The price tag may seem stiff, but lift tickets, lessons or coaching, some kind of off-snow seminar and perhaps a social component are generally included; on multiday curricula, lodging may be included too. For instance, Mt. Bachelor, Oregon, has organized the Hookey Ski Club, which includes reduced-rate lift tickets, discounts on on-mountain service and midweek bus transport from five cities in Oregon and even Idaho. On weekends, the area hosts a similar program for teens called the Pepsi Ski Club. Whether they are for a day, a weekend or a week, such programs therefore fall more in the good-value category than in skiing's bargain bin.

Special packages designed for particular groups combine skiing and social activities at attractive convention rates. In addition to good basic values, companies wishing to market to that particular segment of the population frequently sponsor parties or provide giveaways for all participants. The biennial National Black Summit organized by the National Brotherhood of Skiers takes place at a different major western resort every year. It drew six thousand skiers to Vail in 1993, so you can imagine what great prices such a large organization is able to negotiate for its members. The first National Jewish Singles Ski Week took place in 1995 at Steamboat and the second the following year at Big Sky, Montana. Gay and lesbian skiers converge on Aspen for the annual National Gay Ski Week, while those from the Bay Area flock to the Lake Tahoe Gay and Lesbian Winter Festival and those in the Pacific Northwest head for Whistler's Gay Ski Week.

No special-interest area is growing as quickly as older skiers, and depending on which organization you're looking at, "older" can be defined as fifty and above or eighty and above. The Over the Hill Gang has some four thousand members over the age of fifty in twelve chapters across the

U.S. With the huge and energetic baby boom wave breaking over the five-decade wall, this organization is bound to keep growing. Many ski areas have special OTHG days, about one hundred offer lift-ticket discounts to members and well-priced ski trips and summer vacations. For information, contact OTHG, 3310 Cedar Heights Drive, Colorado Springs, CO 80904; (719) 685-4656.

To the members of the 70+ Ski Club (and its offshoot, the 80+ Ski Club), fifty-year-olds are still kids. Septuagenarians and octogenarians may join for a small lifetime membership fee and get an identification card, a patch and an occasional newsletter. Older skiers should join just out of gratitude, since the club lobbied successfully for free skiing for seniors all over the country. The club's own races and social activities are centered around Hunter Mountain, New York. To join, send five dollars to 70+ Ski Club, 104 East Lake Side Drive, Ballston Lake, NY 12019.

Snowbird, Utah, a mountain that bows to none when it comes to challenge, is the longtime home area of a legendary powder maestro named Junior Bounous. Junior himself is now a senior. His Silver Wings classes for advanced and expert skiers fifty and older attract a loyal corps of locals. He also does Junior's Seniors, a free two-hour program every Tuesday morning in which he guides skiers sixty-two and older around the area and gives complimentary age-appropriate terrain and technique tips. Vacationers are welcome in both programs. Kirkwood's Silver Streaks offers free clinics to any senior skier of intermediate or better ski ability every nonholiday Wednesday morning with the purchase of a lift ticket.

Other areas with a regular seniors' day tend to develop a loyal clientele that skis together. Loon Mountain's Flying 50s charges a modest annual membership fee, for which members can ski for a pittance. The club "meets" two weekday mornings a week. TGIF (Thank Goodness I'm Fifty) takes place every nonholiday Thursday at Attitash/Bear Peak, New Hampshire, and includes a complimentary light breakfast and skill development workshop. Skiers fifty-five and older can join the Wednesday It'Snowonder program at Smugglers' Notch, Vermont, which wraps in morning coffee and donuts and après-ski wine tastings, video analysis, yoga and discussions on pertinent topics around five hours of skiing. Ski Windham, New York, has a Senior Skier Development Program for those fifty-five and older every Tuesday. On Valentine's Day, the area adds a Seniors' Sweetheart day with racing and other events for skiers fifty and older. Whitetail, Pennsylvania, offers low-cost Silver Streaks lift tickets every Wednesday for skiers fifty and older. Copper Mountain is the headquarters for Colorado's Over The Hill Gang, with weekly skis-on "meetings," races and socializing. Breckenridge, Colorado, does a series of 50-Plus Skiing Seminars, while Taos's Masters Ski Weeks for skiers fifty and older draw a club-like cadre of returning skiers. Sun Valley's annual Prime Times ski weeks package lodging, skiing, races and parties. Heavenly Ski Resort, California/Nevada, hosts three-day Seasoned Skiers Workshops once a month and also includes lift tickets, breakfast, lunch, ski instruction and social activities in one price.

Other bargains are organized by geography. Steamboat's All-Cal Ski Weeks in mid-December, for instance, are aimed at Golden Staters, Telluride annually promotes Arizona Days, while Taos Ski Valley hosts the annual Wild Turkey Texas Cup during the first weekend in February, Purgatory hosts God Bless Texas Week in early March and nearby Red River welcomes Louisianans who want to escape New Orleans' Mardi Gras frenzy and instead celebrate coolly in the snowy Southwest. Still other areas show appreciation to people in certain occupations. Hunter Mountain, New York, invites firefighters, police officers, chefs and medical professionals to the slopes for well-priced, fun-filled days of skiing. Silver-Creek, Colorado, puts on an annual "Fireman's Feud," while Purgatory's annual Armed Forces Winter Carnival in late January offers good value and lots of extras to servicemen and women. One popular highlight of each of these special days or weeks is generally a race, in which participants wear their work garb. Loon Mountain, New Hampshire, hosts an annual corporate challenge with racers carrying briefcases. It's no bargain, but it is for charity—and your company may pick up the tab.

CHAPTER TEN

WORK TO SKI

Whether you seek a full-time career in the ski industry, a part-time job to help fund your sport, a way to live in the mountains or a scheme for trading your time for lift tickets, opportunities to cut skiing costs abound. From Junior Patrollers and Junior Instructor positions for teenagers (see "Family Values," page 48) to volunteer slots for retirees, ski country offers many ways to combine vocation and avocation. And if you use a little imagination, you may even be able to create a job of your own and parlay it into skiing privileges.

WORK IN A SKI SHOP

Ski shops all over have places for full- and part-time employees—and especially for seasonal workers to fill in the busy season from early fall to Christmas, and rental specialists use part-timers on Friday evenings and weekend mornings. In addition to pay comparable with other retail establishments, you'll get the inside scoop on the newest equipment and skiwear from suppliers' representatives who visit shops to "clinic" salespeople on technical features. Ski shops also allow their employees to buy products for their own use at a discount. In addition to salespeople and cashiers, shops need and will train equipment technicians to wax and tune skis and eventually to mount and adjust bindings. As long as you have a shop job, you can probably tune your own gear too, and even after you've stopped working there, you'll have the skills to maintain your own equipment properly.

One of the main benefits for shop employees is free or, more commonly, discounted lift tickets. To protect the system from abuse, most areas require at least a letter from a shop manager and identification. Some areas ration the number of employees or the number of skiing days allocated to a specific shop, perhaps by issuing punch cards, which are lent to employees at the shop manager's discretion, good until all the punches are used up. Others ask area ski shops to send lists of employees who ought to get reductions. Still other areas have different policies for full- and part-time employees, or they may limit benefits on weekends and holidays.

A handful of shop owners fund or subsidize ski trips for key employees. The most coveted perk is a chance to attend one of the "on-snow shows" in various parts of the country. Held in January and February, they are the venues where retailers preview and test-ski the upcoming season's equipment. Shops normally send their hardgoods buyers and key salespeople to these events, and some reward salespeople farther down the ladder with a trip, too.

New Jersey's Ski Barn books a major ski trip every spring for employees and their families. The trip is free or subsidized, depending on how long the person has been with Ski Barn, what his or her position is and a variety of other factors. Ski resorts may reward shop employees beyond simply offering discounted lift tickets. The top event is Crested Butte's annual Spring Fling, a party-filled ski week early in April with skiing, shop-against-shop ski racing and a slew of prizes and giveaways. In 1995, a five-day package cost as little as $141 per person including lodging, lift tickets and all the fun stuff.

In addition to the immediate pay and perks, a job in a ski shop is an excellent stepping stone to other positions in the ski industry. Manufacturers and importers of ski equipment and clothing, chains of specialty ski shops or general sporting-goods stores and ski areas of all sizes look for people with interest, enthusiasm and experience in the business of skiing.

WORK AT A SKI AREA

The same local ski areas that are so convenient and inexpensive to visit (see "Hidden Treasures," page 112) also offer a wealth of work opportunities with modest pay and skiing privileges. Small areas usually have a small core of full-time employees, and they build peak-time staffs around them with part-timers. Parking lot attendants, food service workers, cashiers, rental shop workers, snow shovelers and cleaning people don't require much training and are usually needed for a few specific hours each day or evening. Other positions, which require more training and may not provide quite the flexibility in time, include lift-ticket checkers and lift loaders who alternate work time with ski time. Day care workers need to be on duty during ski time, but people on snowmaking and grooming crews work when the lifts are shut down, leaving more time to ski. Small ski hills also offer opportunities to break into ski instruction. Hiring clinics and training sessions teach the fundamentals, and new hires are generally apprenticed to experienced instructors. Working for a small ski area can also be a passport to a good value at a bigger one. Aspen, for instance, has formalized relationships with several Midwestern areas, whose employees, season pass holders and even day skiers receive discounted lift tickets and lodging specials. The ski instructors at these small areas are invited to attend Aspen's annual instructor-training program, with the expectation that they will pass the word about fabulous Colorado skiing to their own mid-American skiers.

Like ski shops, these little local areas not only breed skiers, but they breed people who work their way up in the ski industry. David Ingemie, president of Ski Industries America, which represents hundreds of equipment and clothing manufacturers, importers and distributors, started working part-time at Wachusett Mountain, Massachusetts, when he was still in school.

"REALLY" WORK AT A SKI AREA

To plunge into skiing, to make it your life—for a while, at least—often requires a really big move, and that is to a destination ski resort. Ski bumming is another one of skiing's many time-honored traditions. The term "ski bum" generates an image of a responsibility-free young adult who moves to a ski town and takes a low-level job (or, these days, two or three jobs) to ski or snowboard as much as possible. Some jobs are with the ski area itself—as at small areas, parking lot attendants, food service and rental shop workers, cashiers, lift crews, maintenance workers for buildings and mountain facilities, grooming, crews, snowplow drivers, nursery and day care personnel, patrollers, ski instructors and more. Large areas also need security guards and entire office staffs, which are somehow not usually thought of as "ski bum" positions. On-site restaurants need cooks, servers and bussers, and bars must be tended. Resorts that own hotels and/or manage lodging properties additionally hire doormen, bellmen, front-desk clerks, PBX operators and housekeeping and laundry staffs. Those with convention facilities also hire kitchen workers, people to set up meetings and clean up afterward as well as people to valet-park cars, check coats and serve at banquets. Athletic clubs, skating rinks, teen centers and shops also must be staffed every winter.

Ski areas typically hire seasonal staff in October and November. You'll find newspaper ads in college towns, cities near ski country like Denver and Salt Lake City and resort towns themselves. Because they need hundreds of workers, resorts often hold "job fairs." Usually, they do this on site, but sometimes they also go to nearby cities or likely college towns to recruit for the winter. Top resorts require employees to meet high standards of personal appearance and good grooming, so tame those locks before heading for an interview. For positions that involve interacting with the public, a pleasing and outgoing personality is also a plus. Companies check references, and drug testing for new hires is now common. In raw numbers, the chances of getting a job are good, for big resorts need thousands of seasonal workers. The odds are not always all that great though. Snowbird, Utah, for instance, hires only about 1,100 seasonal workers out of about 4,800 they interview.

The main reason people want to work for a ski area is to get a free season pass (or at least free lift tickets) and the opportunity to ski not just in off-hours, but even in off-minutes when a run or two can be squeezed in. At some areas, however, free skiing is restricted. Snowbird, for instance, limits first-year employees to three free days a season but allows unlimited skiing from the second season on. By contrast, Greek Peak, a small ski resort in upstate New York, allows first-year workers who put in just sixteen hours a week to ski free. Second-year workers ski free, and their entire families are entitled to half-price season passes.

Other common benefits are free ski lessons on a space-available basis, perhaps a lift-ticket discount at other nearby ski areas, discounts on cafeteria meals and often free shuttles from nearby towns if many employees live there. Some areas also offer free or inexpensive on-site day care for employees' children, discounted membership in the resort's health club, gasoline discounts and either an employee store or discounts at the company's retail shops. Payroll deductions, health care plans and retirement programs are variable from area to area and often are linked to full- versus part-time status, tenure and position.

The most coveted jobs in many resort towns are bartending and waiting tables, because the work is at night and the tips can be great. Kitchen work, busing tables and host/hostess slots are other options in the restaurant business. Experienced ski bums are convinced that in addition to the money and skiing, taking home leftovers to feed oneself and one's roommates provides a real side benefit to restaurant work. Housekeepers in hotels and condominiums usually finish their workday in the early afternoon, leaving time to ski and/or work another job. Retail salespeople are needed more during the prime shopping hours after skiing, leaving days free for the slopes. Shuttle-bus drivers work morning, afternoon, day or night shifts, and mechanics are also needed to keep those buses running. If you're looking for this kind of job, you can check the papers and take all the other normal routes, but the easiest way is to attend one of the townwide job fairs, which pop up in late fall.

Most ski towns have some sort of merchant ski pass policy. Local businesses buy discounted season passes to give or more commonly sell at cost to their employees. In many towns, the local chamber of commerce also issues some kind of community card, entitling locals to discounts at member businesses.

ODDBALL JOBS

The range of possible jobs in ski country seems to be endless. State transportation departments and even town road departments in snow country often hire part-time seasonal employees to drive snowplows and sand trucks. Some resorts provide courtesy ski benefits and sometimes even subsidized housing to these heroes who keep the roads open. These jobs usually pay well, but the trade-off is that they usually mean working when the powder is flying. Requirements differ from state to state, but may include a minimum age or special driver's license for heavy equipment or commercial vehicles and will probably include a spotless, or at least a very good, driving record.

Ski resorts also offer a variety of pickup jobs. When a big ski race or major promotion comes to town, companies hire temps to hand out samples or brochures or otherwise help with promotions. Ski photographers and filmmakers often need models. If you polish your skiing, have a good body and a great smile and are cooperative even when asked to do the same move over and over, you can pick up good money for a day or two on the slopes. Ski areas may arm students or other temps with clipboards and questionnaires and send them out on the hill to do on-site market research with skiers during lift rides. This is acknowledged to be a great job, because after each interview, the interviewer has to ski down again to hook up with the next interviewee. Destination ski resorts that attract many foreign guests, particularly from the United Kingdom, sometimes hire on-site representatives, whose job it is to meet groups, help them get settled, preside at a welcome party and be available to answer questions or help solve problems. Breckenridge alone has twelve representatives who work for U.S. companies affiliated with U.K. tour operators.

GET A "REAL" JOB

If you're in for the long haul, think about aiming for a "real" job in a town of unreal beauty and atmosphere. Although jobs at ski areas are generally just those connected with skiing, and resort-related jobs cater to visitors, ski towns are just like other towns in many respects. They need teachers, nurses, police officers, firefighters, municipal employees, newspaper reporters, librarians and all the other people it takes to keep a town going. Of course, the competition is stiff and openings are few, but somebody's got to get the slots, so you might as well apply if you're qualified.

Now Hiring! Ski Resort Jobs, a useful guide to finding jobs in North America's major ski towns, might give you a leg up on your search. It gives nitty-gritty information on when to apply for jobs, season pass policies, what you can expect to be paid and what it costs to live. The book is $14.95 from Perpetual Press, P.O. Box 45628, Seattle, WA 98145; (800) 793-8010.

SKIS-ON JOBS

Of all the work-to-ski jobs, those where work actually involves skiing are ski or snowboard instructor and patroller. These high-profile jobs bring with them prestige—and a nice uniform. The best way to prepare for these positions at a major ski area is to have some experience at a smaller one, as well as previous training and proper certification. Many ski areas conduct tryouts in spring, looking to hire for the following season. For patrollers, training and evaluation is offered in such skills as skiing all kinds of terrain under all kinds of conditions, first aid, toboggan handling, lift evacuation and documentation skills. Instructor hiring clinics concentrate on ski technique, error detection and correction, class handling and communication skills. These clinics may carry a charge, which is normally lower for present employees seeking patrol positions than for the general public.

INSTRUCTION

Ski areas are extremely particular about whom they hire as instructors, and with good reason, for they are one of the main links between new skiers, who might become loyal customers if their experience is good. While some veterans love to teach beginners or children and continue to do so by choice for years, entry-level and kids' classes normally fall to the least experienced instructors. When ski-school directors and supervisors are looking at candidates, they stress that people skills are more important than skiing ability. They can train a good communicator to be a good teacher, but it's not always possible to teach a good skier how to handle people.

Many ski schools, especially small ones, train new hires as instructors. If you get a part-time job, wear the jacket and start teaching, you'll need to aim at least for associate certification from the Professional Ski Instructors of America to move to a full-time job or a larger area. The next step, both in the PSIA process and in any real career move in ski teaching, is full certification. Big areas charge candidates to participate in two- or three-day hiring clinics. Killington inaugurated its School for Instructors in 1970 and now offers three sessions in early winter and one in spring. At nearly three hundred dollars in 1995, Killington's is the most expensive program. Most others are two hundred dollars or less.

Aspiring instructors work with ski-school supervisors and veterans from the area's own ski school and perhaps top-level people from other areas as well. These sessions carry no promise to hire. If you sign up for one, in the best case, you'll get a job somewhere, and at the very least, your skiing will improve after a week or a weekend of dissection and reassembly. Other ski areas holding annual instructor-training courses and/or hiring clinics include Breckenridge, Crested Butte, Indianhead, Jackson Hole, Loon Mountain, Squaw Valley, Stratton Mountain, Sugarloaf/USA, Sun Valley and Vail.

Pay is based on the level of certification and the years of experience a new hire has. Typically, new instructors can expect to earn in the range of ten to twelve dollars an hour or eighty to one hundred dollars per day for a thirty-two- to thirty-six-hour work week. In addition, most ski schools give instructors up to 50 percent of their private-lesson fees. Ski-weekers and private-lesson students often tip as well. In addition to the normal ski-area employee discounts, instructors get good deals on ski equipment. Some pick up extra bucks or free gear by signing on as an "area rep" for an equipment company. The task is to ski on and talk up the brand to students, process direct orders from other instructors and possibly help test new designs. Ski school directors are considered part of most ski areas' management team. For information, contact PSIA, 133 South Van Gordon Street, Lakewood, CO 80228; (303) 987-9390.

PATROLLING

Patrol work is known for long periods of boredom interspersed with moments of great challenge. In addition to such adrenaline-pumping tasks as rescue, trauma care, complex evacuations and avalanche control, patrollers undertake such mundane tasks as planting bamboo poles in the snow to mark hazards, enforcing slow-skiing zones and other rules of the road, posting warning signs and waiting by the radio for a real crisis. Pro patrollers put in long, often grueling, days. The work day starts an hour or more before the lifts open and doesn't end till the last trail is swept for stray skiers. The tasks have to be performed no matter how low the temperatures, how biting the wind or how miserable the snow conditions might be.

The requirements for pro patrolling at a major ski area are stiff. Huge Winter Park, Colorado, for instance, has about fifty full-time paid patrollers who undertake most of the hardcore tasks and one hundred volunteer part-timers and thirty-five or forty junior patrollers who supplement them with crowd control, directing skiers, finding lost skiers and picking up items dropped from lifts. They only play supporting roles in rescues and evacuations. To pass the first step in Winter Park's tryouts, a skier must be able to ski nonstop down first expert runs, earning a high score from a panel of experienced patrollers. Those who pass the skiing test are rigorously interviewed, and when they overcome that hurdle, they must take a one hundred-hour course called Outdoor Emergency Care, oriented toward winter situations and with training at an EMT level.

Joining the volunteer National Ski Patrol System and working at a smaller area is a good way to move toward professional patrolling. At Ski Rio, New Mexico, for instance, volunteers need to be good skiers who have taken the NSPS course in winter first aid before participating in on-hill training, a first-aid refresher and hill evacuation assistance. Junior patrollers must be strong intermediate skiers aged twelve to fifteen who are friendly and articulate and know the mountain. Their tasks are to help senior patrollers and act as a "good Samaritan" to children. In exchange for one weekend a month, volunteers get a season pass.

NSPS courses teach such fundamentals as toboggan handling, how to sweep a trail at day's end and chairlift evacuation. For information on dates, prices and locations, contact NSPS, 133 South Van Gordon Street, Lakewood, CO 80228; (303) 988-1111.

VOLUNTEER FOR FREE SKIING

Ski areas are filled with volunteer possibilities, which are rewarded with free skiing. Some are short-duration commitments. Volunteer to work race crew as a course preparer, gatekeeper or extra hand in the backroom, and you'll get a free ticket, usually good for a full day of skiing at another time. Volunteer for a major event such as a World Cup race, pro race or big freestyle or snowboarding competition, where press-room assistants, VIP hosts and other helpers are needed as well, and you might get a neat hat or even a jacket in addition to your lift ticket. Wildcat, New Hampshire, has a great variety of volunteer slots. In addition to patrollers, hosts and race crew, the area trades skiing for help in instruction and doing evening maintenance.

Many ski areas need volunteers to work one-on-one with physically or

developmentally disabled skiers in their handicap programs. Volunteers
who work fourteen days at Mt. Sunapee, New Hampshire's, physically
challenged program put in four days of training and ten days of teaching
in exchange for a full, unrestricted season pass. Winter Park, the world's
leading center for introducing disabled people to the joys of skiing and is
the site of the National Sports Center for the Disabled, even created a
great volunteer program in which adults and local youngsters who have
no school on Mondays team up to teach developmentally disabled children
how to ski. The adult does the teaching, while the local child who has
signed up to be a Ski Pal is a peer coach who helps get adaptive equipment
ready, plays games, demonstrates skills and becomes a buddy.

With the high-touch philosophy that the ski industry has now em-
braced, volunteer hosts have invaded the mountains. You need to be neat,
personable, friendly, communicative and available to greet and help guests
and occasionally assist with other tasks. In the morning, hosts greet skiers
and help direct them to ticket windows, restrooms, ski lockers or anywhere
else they want to go. At some areas, they help clear sidewalks, park cars,
assist in the rental shop, help out in the children's ski school, work in the
cafeteria at busy times or help a group's on-mountain barbecue run
smoothly. These positions are so popular that some areas, like Mt. Snow,
Vermont, have a waiting list of hopeful hosts.

When they're not assigned other tasks, hosts ski around the mountain
with a pocketful of trail maps in the uniform, ready to assist skiers, notify
the patrol in case of an emergency and generally be congenial and useful
on the mountain. At some areas, volunteer hosts also conduct mountain
tours to help orient new skiers to the area. In exchange for a couple of
days a month, hosts get a free season pass. To prove that skiing is a sport
for all ages, Diamond Peak, Nevada, recruited two dozen retirees for the
resort's host staff. The senior set normally skis free anyway, so they are
definitely in it for the love of the sport.

Sometimes you need to create your volunteer opportunity. Before the
town of Steamboat Springs had established a recycling center, an enterprising local volunteered himself and his truck to haul the ski area's cardboard
to a baler in Denver. He was able to keep bulky discards out of the local
landfill, sell the cardboard at market rates and get a free lift ticket for every
load. Medical personnel willing to be on call in case of an emergency often
get free lift tickets. Massanutten, Virginia, gives emergency-room doctors,
trauma surgeons and their families free skiing if the M.D. arranges to be
available with the ski patrol. EMTs and paramedics who register with the
patrol get similar privileges at many mountains. Skiers with interests in

mountain lore, fauna and flora can find slots as volunteer hosts for the U.S. Forest Service, which manages the land on which most western and a few eastern resorts operate. Cross-country ski centers are the natural habitat for these volunteer rangers, but others conduct naturalist tours at Alpine areas as well. Mammoth Mountain's volunteer naturalist program is exemplary. Some forests even have volunteer patrols to help with back-country winter rescue.

PICK A CAREER THAT INVITES YOU TO SKI

Travel agents enjoy many benefits, including invitations to ski at the world's most glamorous resorts for a fraction of the normal price. A "fam trip," which is short for familiarization trip, is like a mini-ski vacation subsidized by the resort just to give agents a personal look at their facilities. Air travel is reduced to agent rates, and ground arrangements are bargain basement as well. Because resorts want agents to see everything at its best, they lodge them in excellent properties, ferry them around in vans, assign ski hosts to show them around the mountain and wine and dine them royally. The trade-off is most likely a "site inspection" of various hotels and condominium properties.

If travel agents have it good, journalists who write about travel or espe-cially skiing have it even better. Ski magazine writers and editors, newspa-per ski columnists, ski photographers and filmmakers and broadcasters who cover the sport get complimentary lift tickets and often free or reduced lodging, all because resorts want the media to know about them. Print and broadcast journalists who can prove a minimum amount of coverage can apply to North American Ski Journalists Association, which has one na-tional annual meeting and several regional ones each year at reduced rates. And just as resorts invite travel agents on fam trips, they or statewide promotional organizations invite selected media on press trips to ski their mountains. For more information on requirements to join, contact NASJA, P.O. Box 5334, Takoma Park, MD 20913; (301) 864-6428.

SO YOU WANT TO MOVE TO SKI TOWN . . .

Some would say that since landing a job is a lot easier than getting a place to live, a book focusing on the main problem ski bums encounter today would be useful. Finding housing that's not two counties away from work is a real challenge. With the real estate boom in resort centers and now in attractive nearby mountain communities, affordable apartments have virtually disappeared. High-priced resort towns, which is to say those with the best skiing and the most job opportunities, have a critical shortage of employee housing. Workers pay top dollar and yet are often forced into miserably crowded living conditions and/or killer commutes an hour or more from their jobs. In such high-priced, high-profile but relatively isolated resort communities as Aspen, Jackson Hole, Telluride and Vail, there is much more talk about affordable housing than there is action to create enough to meet the need. The bottom line, if you want to move to a ski town, is to save a stash of cash, arrive well before the season starts to find a place to live and *then* look for a job. Once you're more or less established and can tough it out for one winter, the following seasons can be easier. Construction jobs offer good pay during the summer, and the word-of-mouth network may help you find better lodgings for the following ski season. If you really luck out, you'll find a caretaker apartment in one of those fancy vacation homes that are driving up real estate prices while driving workers away. Your references will probably be scrutinized before an owner turns an expensive home over to your care.

Ski bumming can be a lifestyle for a season, a few years or a lifetime. Ski film producer Warren Miller and his buddy Ward Baker spent the winter of 1947 living in a tiny trailer in the Sun Valley parking lot. Warren remembers that they skied one hundred days and spent eighteen dollars apiece that season. Warren has been making ski movies for nearly half-a-century, but in his heart, there's still a place for the ski bum he once was.

CHAPTER ELEVEN

NORDIC FOR NOTHING (OR ALMOST NOTHING

Cross-country is skiing's budget side. Equipment costs less, and just a few lessons can get you on the right technique track. You can cross-country ski wherever there's snow, which may shave travel time and travel costs to a minimum. In addition, private areas' trail-use fees are far less than lift-ticket prices and countless miles of routes on public lands are free. Absolutely free.

Nordic equipment costs a fraction of downhill gear. In 1995, the average price for cross-country gear was $108 for skis, $80 for boots, $33 for bindings and $26 for poles, while Alpine skis averaged $264, boots $231, bindings $128 and poles $33. It doesn't take higher mathematics to see why cross-country is kind to your pocketbook. During the winter of 1995-96, when the most expensive lift ticket in the United States was Aspen's $52, the highest cross-country trail fee was the $19.50 weekend and holiday rate charged by Royal Gorge, California, the nation's largest cross-country area. Royal Gorge boasts eighty-eight trails with a total of 328 kilometers of track, four surface lifts to help novices with some of the uphills and "base" facilities rivaling those at many Alpine ski areas. You can compare the costs another way: a three-night, three-day package including lodging and an interchangeable pass good at North Lake Tahoe's seven cross-country areas started at $134 per person, while the Alpine equivalent started at $229 with skiing at eight areas.

Cross-country pays extra dividends in both fitness and tranquillity. If you go at it with energy, it is as good as running for getting in shape, but it's far easier on the joints. You can also use Nordic skiing simply to relax, for gliding through the quietly beautiful winter countryside will pull you away from the cares of the day. In short, cross-country offers priceless benefits, for you use your own power to move through the snowy woods, across pristine meadows or even up a mountain. Nordic options abound. You can ski on meticulously groomed tracks using the technique of your choice from a quiet shuffle to a power glide, rev up your aerobic engine with the technique called skating or set out into the ungroomed backcountry for the winter equivalent of hiking. Another inexpensive option is showshoe-ing, which also has versions geared to fitness and to simply enjoying fresh air and scenery in winter. Taken together, cross-country and snowshoeing are called "the silent sports."

GEARING UP, NORDIC STYLE

Cross-country equipment has undergone no less than a wholesale revolu-tion since 1993. That's when a ski-maker called Fischer introduced a short new ski, the Revolution. This is a fitting name because it literally caused a revolution in it that trims the learning curve. Short skis also proved to be fun both on tracks and on the ungroomed trails. Soon hybrid mid-length skis made their debut, combining the ease of use of short skis with the stability of traditional long ones. At roughly the same time, other technologies began making their way into the Nordic world. Cap designs were adapted from the Alpine realm for cross-country skis, new boot ma-terials offered both enhanced performance and warmth. These great ad-vances have taken the Nordic world by storm. Enthusiasts began trading up, with the result that a lot of technically obsolete but still usable equip-ment has made its way to ski shops' bargain bins and ski swaps. If you are a new cross-country skier looking for gear, you'll have to make a decision: Do you go with the best of the new with the understanding that it will enhance your enjoyment of the sport, or do you look first at the price tag and buy budget stuff?

Clothing for cross-country is normally also less expensive than for Al-pine, and it is more versatile as well. Although serious racers wear tight Lycra suits, recreational skiers can use the kind of activewear they'd select for winter running or hiking. Before you outfit yourself for your new sport, take inventory of your stock of longjohns, wool socks, tights, fleece jackets, windshirts and windpants, warm vests, hats, headbands and the like. You'll be surprised at how much you can assemble into a cross-country outfit, especially if you layer to accommodate changes in the weather and your own heating and cooling cycles as you alternate skiing and resting.

A further wrinkle in the equipment scene is that cross-country skiing is far more weather-vulnerable than Alpine. Therefore, in the wake of a poor snow year (for example, 1994-95 in the East and Midwest), you're likely to find real bargains in equipment and clothing. In addition to traditional ski shops, outdoor, camping and mountaineering retailers often specialize in Nordic gear.

GETTING STARTED

A popular Nordic saying is "If you can walk, you can ski." And so you can, after a fashion. To be an efficient and comfortable skier, a few lessons are recommended, but most beginners find the sport easier to learn than Alpine skiing or snowboarding. Cross-country centers offer lessons, as do many local recreation and outdoor education programs and local chapters or hiking and mountaineering clubs such as the Appalachian Mountain Club, Colorado Mountain Club and Sierra Club. In addition, January 1996 marked the first Ski Fest, a free introduction and equipment-demo program. Scores of Nordic centers across the continent provided a chance to try the new short skis, which make cross-country so easy to learn, and to receive basic instruction. Participation is free, but you must register. For information on sites, contact Ski Fest, 259 Bolton Road, Winchester, NH 02370; (603) 239-8888.

WHERE TO SKI

In theory, you can cross-country ski anywhere that has adequate snow cover, and enthusiastic Nordic skiers will travel to seek out the best places. In practice, many new and occasional cross-country skiers will choose where they ski according to the type of Nordic skiing they prefer and, of course, where they live. If you live in the snowbelt, you have many nearby choices. If you don't, you'll have to travel, much as Alpine skiers do.

GOOD GROOMING

The most expensive trail fees are usually at large, dedicated cross-country centers, which make a fetish of grooming and trail preparation and draw track skiers and skaters. They epitomize the philosophy of "you get what you pay for." They provide outstanding facilities, normally a choice of tracks etched into the snow for traditional skiing and smooth lanes for skating, as well as ski schools, large stocks of rental equipment, a substantial and well-equipped main lodge and often warming huts along the trail system. Alpine areas often run nearby Nordic centers, offering a change of pace for downhill skiers and something for "nonskiers" to do. There usually is a trail fee but it is often lower than a comparably sized and located Nordic-only area, perhaps because cross-country and Alpine skiers share some of the base facilities. Some Alpine areas, including Ski Sunlight, Colorado, and Schweitzer Mountain Resort, Idaho, have opted not to charge for use of their cross-country trails.

When the snow falls on golf courses and municipal or state parks, you can often find very inexpensive and convenient cross-country opportunities. Sometimes, the agency that manages the park or volunteers from the local Nordic club will set tracks whenever the snow falls. At other times, skiers simply glide across the snow, finding their own paths and making their own tracks. It's not just the small, strictly hometown skiing that's free. Sometimes, the most glamorous and expensive resorts offer Nordic skiing at no cost at all. The seventy-five kilometers of groomed trails lacing over fifteen square miles in and around Aspen, for instance, are free. The Aspen Nordic Club maintains the trail system as a service to locals and visitors. And Telluride, which has become so chic that promoters spend all their time explaining that the town hasn't become an Aspen, has thirty cross-country kilometers that are also free.

It is also worth noting that Nordic skiing is one area where the Midwest needn't have an inferiority complex. Long cold winters, abundant snow cover, rolling terrain and a population of winter-sports enthusiasts combine to make cross-country a top sport. Minnesota's Gunflint Trail (800-338-6932) is a vast network of routes punctuated with lodges and cross-country ski areas. The Lake Superior North Shore Ski Trail (Lutsen Chamber of Commerce, 218-663-7804) stretches over small mountains and through pine forests in Minnesota's far north. Wisconsin's Birkebeiner system (715-634-2908) is one of the country's premier Nordic networks and site of the best-known ski marathon in the U.S. Other individual cross-country centers are the peer of any in the land.

Dude and guest ranches and some snowbelt resort hotels have gone into Nordic skiing in a big way. They frequently have enormous and well-run Nordic facilities, free for guests and modestly priced for others. Colorado's C Lazy U (970-887-3344), Home Ranch (970-879-1780), Latigo Ranch (800-227-9655) and Vista Verde (800-526-7433); Idaho's Rocky Mountain Ranch (208-327-7444) and Wapiti Meadow Ranch (208-382-4336); and Montana's Lone Mountain Ranch (406-995-4644) are among the top guest ranches that offer extensive trail networks and real cross-country programs. Such luxury resorts with expansive grounds as the Lodge at Cordillera (800-548-2721), Colorado; Grouse Mountain Lodge, Montana; The Equinox and the Woodstock Inn, Vermont; and the Balsams/Wilderness (800-255-0600) and Bretton Woods, both in New Hampshire, offer free use of their extensive Nordic systems to guests.

Colorado's Snow Mountain Ranch (970-887-2152) is in a class by itself for budget skiers because it combines economical lodging with exceptional cross-country terrain. Montana's Izaak Walton Lodge (406-688-5700), on the edge of Glacier National Park, appeals equally to railroad buffs and Nordic aficionados. The Northeast is rich in other small country inns, and many of them likewise offer free skiing to their guests and also welcome the general public to their trail systems. Among the many such lodges are Maine's Bethel Inn (207-824-6276); Vermont's Mountaintop Inn (800-445-2100) and Viking Guest House and Touring Center (802-824-3933); New York's Adirondak Loj (518-523-3441) and Bark Eater (518-576-2221); and Quebec's Far Hill's Inn (800-567-6636) and La Montagne Coupée (514-886-3845). In the Pacific Northwest, Sun Mountain Lodge (800-572-0493) and Mazama Country Inn (800-422-3048) are two of the warm, wonderful lodgings along the 175-kilometer trail system that snakes through the scenic Methow Valley (800-422-3048 in Washington State; 509-996-2148 out of state).

THE CALL OF THE WILD

Our tax dollars buy us a lot of wonderful skiing. Western skiers in particular treasure the abundant free trails that lace through wilderness and near-wilderness land administered by the U.S. Forest Service, the National Park Service and the Bureau of Land Management. The park service, which sometimes does charge winter entry fees to certain popular parks, grooms and tracksets some trails. The most noteworthy are Yosemite and Yellowstone. Other trails on public lands are more likely to be marked but not groomed. Opportunities present themselves in surprising ways. For Twin City skiers, for instance, the Minneapolis Zoo is a popular excursion; regular zoo admission is charged both for the chance to ski and the opportunity to see the animals.

Growing networks of high-country lodgings makes the backcountry accessible to most reasonably fit Nordic skiers. Huts have their roots in the Alps, but in North America, their styles range from simple cottages and A-frames to relatively lavish log structures. Yurts, derived from nomadic Mongolians' dwellings, are round, tent-like structures built on platforms. Overnighting in a hut or yurt is inexpensive. Amenities are usually limited to such basics as tables, benches that may also be used as sleeping platforms, mattresses or pads, a stove and cooking equipment, firewood and electric lighting, but there will probably be a privy. You must bring in your own sleeping bag, food and personal gear. Reservations are mandatory and should be made well in advance for weekends and full moons. Some of the top hut systems in the country include Colorado's Alfred A. Braun Memorial Hut (reservations through the Tenth Mountain Division Hut System), Hinsdale Haute Route (970-944-2269), Mountain Creek Ranch (970-789-1834), Never Summer Nordic Yurts (970-482-9411), San Juan Hut Systems (970-728-6935), Summit Huts & Trails Assn. (reservations though the Tenth Mountain Division Hut System) and Tenth Mountain Division Hut System (970-925-5775). Colorado's Paragon Guides (970-926-5299), New York's Adirondack Hut Tours (518-828-7007) and Washington's Rendezvous Outfitters (800-422-3048) are among the guide services organizing hut-to-hut tours.

In addition to the hut systems run as private enterprises or by not-for-profit organizations, the U.S. Forest Service has rustic backcountry cabins in such states as Alaska, Idaho and Montana. For information on the existence and availability of these cabins, contact regional USFS regional or ranger district offices (found in the phone book under U.S. Government).

NORDIC WORK AND VOLUNTEER OPPORTUNITIES

If work-to-ski appeals to you but you're a Nordic nut, check with mountaineering and outdoor stores to see if they are hiring retail or back-shop workers. Cross-country centers and Nordic inns are also good bets. They essentially need the same kind of staff as Alpine areas, including food service, rental shop, instructors and patrol staff but probably excluding parking lot attendants and lift personnel. Hut systems may employ hut-keepers, a job that appeals to those who love backcountry isolation. Volunteer opportunities also abound. Every Nordic club can use volunteers to help with trail work, coaching or children's programs and races and other special events. In some cases, the Forest Service or local agencies may have openings for volunteer hosts to lead interpretive ski tours.

THE OTHER WINTER ACTIVITY

Snowshoeing is a low-key relative of cross-country skiing. It enables people to explore—on big, flat feet—the winter backcountry, where nature dozes under a blanket of white. Ground plants are buried, trees wear a snowy mantle, many birds have migrated and many furry creatures hibernate. Others are at their winter feeding grounds where they are often easier to spot than in summer. Deer, elk and moose come out for winter feed, and coyotes and foxes sometimes can be spotted searching for prey. Smaller creatures, which we take for granted in summer, scurry about, and even when we don't see them, we spot tracks showing where they've been scampering.

Snowshoeing is an easy and exceptionally inexpensive way to be part of this world. The activity requires little training, and snowshoes require a onetime investment of about seventy-five dollars to one hundred fifty dollars. Once you've bought the shoes, learned how to put them on and become accustomed to a big-foot gait, you're a snowshoer. You can choose your snowshoeing goals and pick your pace from gonzo uphills on small running shoes, which have more to do with fitness than with wilderness, to arduous backcountry excursions on large, load-bearing behemoth shoes suitable for winter campers. For experiencing the beauty and tranquillity of winter, midsized snowshoes and trails through forests make an unbeatable combination.

In addition to snowshoes, which can be rented from most outdoor retailers, some ski shops and many cross-country ski centers, you need to be prepared with warm, layered clothing, water-resistant hiking boots or other winter footwear, gaiters to keep your feet warm and dry, sunscreen and a water bottle. Most showshoers use ski poles for walking rhythm and balance.

Most snowshoers go off into the woods by themselves, but it is an activity that lends itself perfectly to guided naturalist tours. Such a trip can be an eye-opener in terms of winter ecology, and you'll never see winter the same way again. Snowshoeing is inherently a low-key sport, but it is found in various contexts from free tours in national or state parks to pricey itineraries with fancy box lunches organized by top ski resorts.

CHAPTER TWELVE

SOMETHING EXTRA

A special service or a luxury touch can make the difference between an ordinary ski trip and a memorable one. These little extras may be free, or they may be worth the cost in terms of simply making you feel wonderful. Imagine how lovely it is when you come off the mountain on a stormy day to find that someone has brushed the snow off your windshield or cleaned your headlights. Here's a sampling of some other added touches you'll find at North American ski resorts.

- The Aspen Skiing Company, which operates four ski areas around Aspen, is so anxious to get the word of its wonderful skiing out that it'll supply you with free postcards. Stop at any ticket office, write your cards and the company will even pay the postage.
- If you stay in a Crested Butte, Colorado, condominium at Christmas, you'll find a ready-to-trim tree, compliments of the resort.
- Drop your skis off at the bottom of any of Aspen's four mountains at the end of the day, and claim them the next day at any other mountain for two dollars.
- The Glenwood Springs Hostel, Colorado, keeps a small stock of skiwear and accessories to lend to guests who have forgotten something at home.
- Free cookies and hot apple cider are available from nine A.M. to eleven A.M. at the top of Snowmass, Colorado's Coney Glade lift.
- At Beaver Creek, Colorado, the free snack is cookies and hot chocolate, served daily at four P.M. at the pedestrian mall.
- Keystone, Colorado, lends complimentary beepers to parents whose babies and small children are in the Child Care Center.
- The Grocery Company of Steamboat Springs can stock your condo kitchen before you arrive so that you don't have to spend your first

day shopping. Mail your shopping list to them at P.O. Box 2669, Steamboat Springs, CO 80477, or fax it to (970) 879-4186.

- Lunches at Suicide Six, Vermont, are prepared at the luxurious Woodstock Inn and delivered fresh to the base lodge.
- While other ski areas may staff an Activities Desk to assist skiers, Beaver Creek, Colorado, has a concierge, just as in the most elegant hotels in the world.
- Breakfast in Bed will deliver a hot breakfast from any restaurant in Winter Park, Colorado, to your condo or hotel.
- You can escape the cold in heated cars on Killington, Vermont's SkyShip gondola.
- If you've done a little too much après-skiing, avail yourself of Tipsy Taxi, a free service available in many ski towns to ensure the safety of visitors and residents alike. Your bartender will be happy to call for you.
- Mountain Caterers, based at Heavenly Valley, California/Nevada, delivers gourmet lunches, including fruit and cracker trays, entrées, wine and dessert, to skiers looking for a romantic midday escape. These picnics are served at secluded mountain locations with great views.
- Businesspeople who can't totally get away during a day or evening on the slopes appreciate Ski Windham, New York's, slopeside business center.
- In the Vail Valley, you can rent a humidifier (970-476-3374) for your room, a walkie-talkie (970-949-0803) to take to the slopes or a hot tub (970-949-6339) for the terrace of your condo.
- You can have your cookies and ski too during SilverCreek, Colorado's Girl Scout Cookie Ski n' Sample Days in late February. After you've tasted the treats, you're welcome to buy boxes of them at the Sterling Base Lodge.
- The thoughtful ski valets at Deer Valley, Utah, remove your skis from your car rack and guard them while you park.

TOLL-FREE NUMBERS

For basic destination information, start with the toll-free information and reservations numbers below (when an area does not have an 800 number, the general information number is given). For some types of information, such as ski information or snow-conditions reports, you may be directed to another number, and this second number might or might not be a toll call, but at least you can start your research for free. In addition, regional resorts' 800 numbers may not be accessible from distant parts of the country, and sometimes an 800 number is not available in-state. As with every other price or parameter in this book, the phone numbers below were valid when they were written and are subject to change.

Alpine Meadows, CA	(800) 441-4423
Alyeska, AK	(800) 880-3880
Angel Fire, NM	(800) 446-8117
Ascutney, VT	(800) 243-0011
Aspen, CO	(800) 290-1325
Attitash, NH	(800) 223-SNOW
The Balsams/Wilderness, NH	(800) 255-3400
Bear Valley, CA	(800) 736-6203
Beaver Creek, CO	(800) 622-3131
Belleayre, NY	(800) 431-4555
	(central Catskills reservations)
Big Boulder, PA	(800) 468-2442
The Big Mountain, MT	(800) 858-5439
Big Sky, MT	(800) 548-4486
Bogus Basin, ID	(800) 367-4397
Bolton Valley, VT	(800) 451-5025 *(condo reservations)*
	(800) 451-3220 *(lodge reservations)*
Bousquet, MA	(413) 443-9186
Breckenridge, CO	(800) 800-BREC *(lodging)*;
	(800) 221-1091 *(lodging/air packages)*
Bretton Woods, NH	(603) 278-1000
Brian Head, UT	(800) 272-7426
Bridger Bowl, MT	(800) 223-9609
Brodie Mountain, MA	(413) 443-4752
Bromley, VT	(800) 865-4786
Brundage Mountain, ID	(800) 888-7544
Burke Mountain, VT	(800) 922-BURK
Butternut, MA	(413) 528-4433
Caberfae, MI	(616) 862-3333
Camelback, PA	(717) 629-1661
Canaan Valley, WV	(800) 662-4121

Cannon Mountain, NH	(603) 823-5563
Cochran, VT	(802) 434-2479
Copper Mountain, CO	(800) 458-8386
Cranmore, NH	(800) SUN-N-SKI
Crested Butte, CO	(800) 544-8448
Dartmouth Skiway, NH	(603) 643-4300
Deer Valley, UT	(800) 424-DEER
Diamond Peak, NV	(800) GO-TAHOE
Discovery Basin, MT	(800) 443-2381
Eldora Mountain Resort, CO	(303) 440-8700
Gore Mountain, NY	(518) 251-GORE
Grand Geneva, WI	(414) 248-8811
Grand Targhee, WY	(800) TARGHEE
Gray Rocks, QU	(800) 567-6767
Great Divide, MT	(406) 449-3746
Greek Peak, NY	(800) 955-2SKI
Gunstock, NH	(800) GUNSTOCK
Heavenly Ski Resort, CA/NV	(800) 2-HEAVEN
Holiday Valley, NY	(800) 323-0020
Hunter Mountain, NY	(800) 775-4641
Indianhead, MI	(800) 3-INDIAN
Jack Frost Mountain, PA	(800) 468-2442
Jackson Hole, WY	(800) 443-6931
Jay Peak, VT	(800) 451-4449
Jiminy Peak, MA	(413) 738-5500
Keystone, CO	(800) 222-0188
Killington, VT	(800) 621-MTNS
King Pine, NH	(800) FREE-SKI
Kirkwood, CA	(800) 967-7500
Lake Louise, AB	(800) 661-4141
Lake Tahoe, CA/NV	(800) TAHOE-4-U *(North Shore)*
	(800) AT-TAHOE *(South Shore)*
Loon Mountain, NH	(800) 229-STAY *(on-mountain)*
	(800) 227-4191
Lost Trail, MT	(406) 821-3211
Loveland, CO	(800) 736-3SKI *(ski area)*
	(800) 225-LOVE *(lodging)*
Mad River Glen, VT	(802) 496-3551
Mammoth, CA	(800) 367-6752
Massanutten, VA	(800) 229-6582
Maverick Mountain, MT	(406) 834-3454
Middlebury College Snow Bowl, VT	(802) 388-7951
Monarch, CO	(800) 332-3668
Montana Snowbowl, MT	(800) 728-2695
Mont Orford, QU	(800) 567-7315
Mont Ste.-Anne, QU	(800) 463-1568
Mt. Airy Lodge Ski Resort, PA	(800) 441-4410

Mt. Bachelor, OR	(800) 829-2442
Mt. Baker, WA	(206) 734-6771
Mt. Norquay/Mystic Ridge, AB	(403) 752-4421
Mt. Rose, NV	(702) 849-0704
Mt. Snow/Haystack, VT	(800) 245-SNOW
Mt. Washington Valley, NH	(800) 367-3364
Northstar, CA	(800) GO-NORTH
Okemo, VT	(800) 78-OKEMO
The Pass*, WA	(800) 528-1234
Pico, VT	(800) 989-PICO
Purgatory, CO	(800) 525-0892
Ragged Mountain, NH	(603) 768-4575
Red Lodge, MT	(800) 444-8977
Red River, NM	(800) 331-7669
Reno, NV	(800) FOR-RENO
Royal Gorge, CA	(800) 500-3871,
	(800) 666-3871 *(from northern California)*
Saddleback, ME	(800) MOMENTS
Sandia Peak/Albuquerque, NM	(800) 473-1000
Schweitzer Mountain, ID	(800) 8311-8810
Showdown, MT	(800) 433-0022
SilverCreek, CO	(800) 448-9458
Silver Star, BC	(800) 663-4431
Sipapu, NM	(800) 587-2240
Ski Apache, NM	(800) 253-2255
Ski Cooper, CO	(800) 933-3901
Ski Liberty, PA	(717) 642-8288
Ski New Hampshire	(800) 88-SKI-NH
Ski 93, NH	(800) WE-SKI-93
Ski Rio, NM	(800) 2-ASK-RIO
Ski Roundtop, PA	(717) 432-9631
Ski Santa Fe, NM	(800) 777-CITY
Ski the Summit, CO	(800) 842-8069
Ski Windham, NY	(800) SAY-SKIW
Smugglers' Notch, VT	(800) 451-8752
Snowbasin, UT	(801) 399-1135
Snowbird, UT	(800) 453-3000
Snowmass, CO	(800) 215-7669
Snowshoe/Silver Creek, WV	(304) 572-5252
Squaw Valley USA, CA	(800) 545-4350
Steamboat, CO	(800) 525-BOAT
Stowe, VT	(800) 24-STOWE,
	(800) 253-4SKI
Stratton, VT	(800) THE-MTNS
Sugar Bowl, CA	(916) 426-3651
Sugarbush, VT	(800) 53-SUGAR
Sugarloaf, ME	(800) THE-LOAF

Suicide Six, VT	(800) 448-7900
Sunday River, ME	(800) 543-2SKI
Sun Peaks, BC	(800) 807-3257
Sunshine, AB	(403) 762-6500,
	(800) 661-1676 *(Canada)*
Sun Valley, ID	(800) 634-3347
Tahoe North Convention &	(800) 824-6348
Visitors Bureau, CA/NV	
Taos Ski Valley, NM	(800) 776-1111
Telluride, CO	(800) 525-3455
Temple Mountain, NH	(603) 924-6949
Timberline, WV	(800) SNOWING
Vail, CO	(800) 525-2257
Waterville Valley, NH	(800) GO-VALLEY
Whistler, BC	(800) WHISTLER
Whitetail, PA	(717) 328-9400
Wildcat, NH	(800) 255-6439
Winter Park, CO	(800) 729-5813

* Alpental-Snoqualmie-Ski Acres-Hyak

INDEX